Been There, Done That

Volume II

Angie Brady

Copyright © 1998 by Angela Brady

Library of Congress
Catalog Card No. TX-4-597-663

ISBN 09662743—1—8

All rights reserved. No part of this book may be reproduced in any manner without written permission from the publisher.

Printed in the United States of America

Published by Tysseland Publications
762 S. Rosemont St.
Mesa, Arizona 85206

First Edition 1998

ACKNOWLEDGMENTS

My sister, Marie Saterbak, for the story she wrote, "White Organdy Dresses."

My husband, Bill, without whose unwavering support, this book could not have been published.

Kathy Paulson, for her patience and proficiency in deciphering and editing my writing.

Readers of Been There, Done That for encouraging me to write another book.

DEDICATION

To my grandchildren

Matthew, Morgan, Nicole, David,

Douglas and Kayla Jenkins

CONTENTS

Preface	i
The Magic Box	1
Coupon Clippings	5
Hugs, Kisses and Handshakes	7
Just For Today	9
You're Lucky If . . .	10
Perfect Gifts for Your Children	11
A New Cookbook	13
Dance, Anyone?	14
Hair Hassles	15
Another Life to Live	17
A Woman of Color and Class	21
The Gulf War	23
A Stole With Class	25
Windpower	27
The Runaway	29
Destruction	30
Feet	31
Excuses	33
Reflections	35
Of Spun Gold	37
Another Miracle	39
Dishwashing	41
Accident Prone	43
Seize the Moment	45
Is Bigger Better?	47
Forging Friendships	49
Remembrances of Christmas Past	51
Vacation, A Rededication to Life	53
Faith	55
Eyes	57
Mad Hens	59
Copper Boilers	61

The Reunion	63
My Rose Garden	65
Computers and Me	67
If You . . .	68
Earrings	69
After the Dance	71
Rapport	73
Fingernails	75
One Woman's Hands	76
Plagued by Perfection	77
Rainy Day Blessings	79
Rain	81
The County Fair	83
White Organdy Dresses	85
My Surprising Sister	91
Living a Nightmare	93
A Red Box of Memories	95
Treading on Thin Ice	97
No	99
Another Birthday Peek	100
Of Lilacs and Punishment	101
Weathering the Weather	103
Do Pictures Lie?	105
Whatever Happened to Aprons?	107
Laughter	109
One of a Pair	111
In Praise of TV	113
Your First Gray Hair	115
Another Four-Letter Word	117
Potato Days	119
Compliments	121
A Purse for Every Outfit	123
Dressed for the Occasion	125
Early Birds	127
Between Sips	129
Tablecloths	131

Sweet Scents	133
Lost and Found	135
Two Dear Deer	139
Cheers for Coffee	141
The Ax Murder	143
Why Worry?	145
Tears	147
Theaters, Then and Now	149
From Sunrise to Sunset	153
Automatic Writing	154
Snoring	155
Your Stingy If You . . .	157
Waiting	158
Just Dump It	159
The Painting	161
Another Moving Day	163
Genetic Photography	165
Treatise on T-shirts	167
In Retrospect	169
Through My Window	170
Just Another Day	171
A New Life Unfolding	175
My First Prayer	179

PREFACE

Publishing a book is akin to having your first baby. It is exciting and frightening. You are thrust into unknown territory without preparation. You wonder, *now what?*

The "It can't be me" syndrome permeates your brain. You, an author? How dare you venture into the publishing world? Is it ridiculous fantasy?

The creativity which flows so freely during your 5 a.m. appointment with your pencil suddenly has frozen into place. Like lava.

True, islands have been created from lava. But you feel suspended—neither here, nor there.

Line by line, you proof your manuscript until your thumbs tingle from turning the pages.

Finally, you pack your manuscript into a box, much as you packed your suitcase, leaving it by the front door, weeks before leaving for the hospital to have your first born. Unlike the pink and blue layette, your manuscript is black on white paper.

You have abdominal cramps—like the contractions during labor.

You carefully carry your manuscript to the printer. You are told it may take a month to six weeks to publish it.

You pace the floor. You wonder what it will look like with its three-dimensional lettering, *Been There, Done That* on its brilliant blue cover.

You sleep fitfully, worrying if every comma is in place. Every period. Every picture.

Finally, the phone call you have been waiting for.

"Yes, yes, I'll pick them up."

You are exhausted as you cradle your first book in your arms. You wonder about its future. But for now, you relax—happy your book is born.

Slowly, you hear friends and acquaintances are reading your book. You are thrilled and thankful to hear them say they both laughed and cried as they read it. Just as you did when you wrote it.

You are invited to read and sign at women's groups, at libraries and bookstores. You remember your mother's coaching when you, as a youngster, read at Luther League or a 4-H Club meeting. You wish she were here to tell you to speak more slowly and don't forget the pause. But you know she is too busy as God's grammarian so you are on your own. You notice, as you read, that your book takes on a life of its own.

You, same as a mother of a toddler, forget the discomfort of pregnancy and the pangs of labor, begin thinking of writing another book. Each morning you pick up your pencil and write. *Been There, Done That Volume 2*; you plan a purple cover.

You pray the book's message is positive and uplifting. You thank God for this wonderful experience as you place your new baby—your book—in His hands.

THE MAGIC BOX

Radio, during its heyday, made absorbing entertainment. Voices wafted as magic through the airwaves and came through a box in our living room.

And what a box it was! The most beautiful piece of furniture in our home, fashioned like a desk, its battery stored in the bottom drawer.

Summer afternoons, I, riveted to the radio, listened to the soap operas. Truly, these programs were sponsored by the soap companies. *Pepper Young's Family, Ma Perkins, Judy and Jane* and *Backstage Wife* were soap-worthy.

My favorite program, *Little Orphan Annie*, prompted me to ask my parents to adopt a sister for me from the Lake Park Children's Home. Because this didn't materialize, Orphan Annie became my fantasy sister. I raced a mile and a half home from school to hear the program at 4:45. Although Hitler was rampaging throughout Europe, I missed the satire that Orphan Annie was adopted by Daddy Warbucks. Ah, the bliss of childhood!

My favorite actor, Orson Welles, in his deep dramatic voice, presented a Halloween prank about an invasion from Mars on Oct. 30, 1938. The play was titled "The War of the Worlds". To me, it was only a play because CBS interrupted the program several times to state it was pure fiction. Headlines the next day told of thousands calling police and radio stations. Fearing death and destruction, many families in New Jersey and New York fled their homes. An embarrassed CBS apologized to a near panicked nation.

Cecil B. DeMille's resonant voice announced, "Lux Presents Hollywood." Memories of Agnes Moorhead on *Lux Radio Theatre* in "Sorry, Wrong Number" still sends chills up my spine. Talented stars of stage and screen such as Helen Hayes, Tyrone Power, Loretta Young and Barbara Stanwyck made winter snowbound evenings, complete with Dad's popcorn, a delight.

Although I had never seen a movie, I had a large black scrapbook full of pictures of movie stars snipped with my scissors from Mother's magazines. I'm unsure what happened to this collection.

I heard Mae West tell the dummy, Charlie McCarthy, on the *Chase and Sanborn Hour*, to "Come up and see me sometime." I didn't understand this conversation.

You Bet Your Life with Groucho Marx and his rapid, unrehearsed, machine gun type of humor, held my father spellbound. My folks also enjoyed *The Jack Benny Show* and *Fibber McGee & Molly*. Mother always identified with Fibber McGee's closet, the closet so full that when the door opened, things came tumbling out. She also said the 10 o'clock news helped her keep up with what was going on in the world.

And what events did go on. In 1936 the networks covered King Edward VIII when he announced his abdication as King of England, after less than a year as king, ". . . in order to marry the woman I love." It was a brief but deeply human message.

The networks also covered its first presidential race. It was between FDR and Alfred Landon. My dad was for FDR and I for Landon. This made interesting table conversation.

I dreamed of becoming a radio personality, dressed in a black evening gown with jewels, standing by a microphone dropping my script to the floor as I spoke.

I'd dress in whatever sophisticated clothes I could find in Mother's trunk and read poetry into my "mike," an empty spool of thread. Sometimes, my cousin and I tied grocery string between two tin cans and we could hear each other from one room to another. Real radio.

Total magic, this Golden Age of Radio, which provided news and entertainment for small towns and large cities across America. I miss it.

COUPON CLIPPINGS

Coupons are guaranteed to make me feel like a spendthrift. Even worse, lazy.

Every Sunday paper is resplendent with coupons for foods I've never tasted or desired to taste—precooked pastas and devilish desserts, peanut butter, jams and cereals. However, I have shelves of peanut butter and cereal and we eat little jam.

I toss the offending sheet in the garbage with a fine feeling of freedom.

Until the guilt sets in, when I read about women who take couponing seriously, saving hundreds, even thousands, of dollars a year. They shop exclusively at stores which double or triple their coupons. The guilt becomes even more acute when I read many have established college funds for their children and grandchildren from the money saved by couponing.

I read they have alphabetized coupon holders and allocate several hours weekly for adding new coupons and plucking out the outdated ones.

Some belong to coupon trading clubs. I imagine them eating mini-muffins and drinking coffee latte bought with coupons.

So I tried couponing for a month, saving every coupon with any food I could possibly visualize using. I placed them in labeled envelopes for easy access. Then I spent an hour sorting coupons before leaving for the grocery store.

My usual twenty-minute shopping took an hour-and-a-half. Even early on Monday morning, I was surprised to find other coupon laden folks like myself. The store stocked only half my coupons so I went to another supermarket five miles away (the one with which I wasn't familiar).

Hunting another two hours, I redeemed all my coupons. I saved $18.50 that day for a total preparation and shopping time of four-and-a-half hours and twelve miles on my car.

Exhausted, I rested forty-five minutes before gaining enough energy to unpack my groceries.

Therefore, I concluded coupon clipping isn't my forte. I'll leave it for the more organized folks and learn to stifle my feelings of guilt when the sheaves of coupons arrive with the Sunday paper.

I may even work off my guilt by hitting a golf ball.

HUGS, KISSES AND HANDSHAKES

You are by nature, a hugger, kisser, handshaker or none of the above. Your hands, as distant cousins who have never met, may hang limp at your side when you see an acquaintance or the former "best friend" from your childhood. Worse, you may keep those hands in your pockets. Worse yet, you shake hands with a limp noodle handshake. Even deadlier, you shake hands using an arthritic bone-crushing grip.

You are cognizant of what kind of hands on-hands off creature you are. But do you have the social skills or common sense when to use what?

Do you blindly hug everyone? Kiss everyone—including babies when you have never even thought of running for office? Or, perish those wicked thoughts, do you encourage both hugging and kissing at the same time?

Perhaps you, a non-kisser, turn your face away as a welcoming social peck on the cheek ends at your ear. Or you lower your head so the kiss aimed at your mouth ends on your forehead. Or, horror of horrors, on the tip of your nose. Unhygienic at best, it may spread a cold, flu or worse.

Hugging, your lipstick may smear a shirt, tie or shoulder. A stain sure to be noticed. Especially by wives.

Strange, your lipstick may rub off in a millisecond as you greet your husband at the door; whereas, it may take more than an hour to remove it from another man's clothing.

The height of embarrassment is hugging a stranger. "Sorry, I thought you were Eunice."
Ever try waving?

JUST FOR TODAY

Put others first.
Accept their indiscretions.
Write a congratulatory note.
Forget fattening food.
Don't brood over small slights.
Use your best china for family,
with the finest linen,
and silver.
Treat your family as your guests.
Treat yourself as a guest.
Wear your new dress with pride.
Wear a smile.

YOU'RE LUCKY IF . . .

You have enough milk for breakfast.
You remember to pay income tax.
You have enough money to pay the tax.
The rain stops as you go out the door.
It starts again when you are in the car.
The telemarketer hangs up on you.
You wake up before the alarm.
Your petunias survive a first frost.
You survive the blizzard.

PERFECT GIFTS FOR YOUR CHILDREN

This Christmas give your children gifts which need no packaging. No ribbons. No postage.

Gifts such as trust, acceptance, and compassion are free—gifts from your soul—perfect gifts.

Trust your children's integrity, their ability to turn mistakes into triumphs. Learn to recognize those triumphs.

Accept their personal idiosyncrasies even as your parents accepted yours. Allow them to follow their own star and to grow at their own pace.

Ladle the gift of compassion wisely and freely. When their life goes wrong, help them cross the street of forgiveness and gift them love.

Expect them to grow into men and women able to assume the awesome responsibilities of the next millennium.

Expect not your clones.

A NEW COOKBOOK

A new cookbook is enchanting. It's guaranteed to fill delightful hours paging through it.

Pictures abound. They range from sticky rolls resplendent with pecans to a plate of appetizers on a glass platter. These delicacies photographed in a luxurious dining room. Fit for a queen.

Recipes for cookies range from the modest molasses cookies Mother baked to the latest gourmet thousand calorie chocolate nut and coconut bars.

The salads intrigue me. From the red, white and blue 4th of July gelatin salads, to potato salads where the only recognizable ingredient is the potato, to rice salads in various stages of glorification.

I page to the casseroles. On page sixty-two, they are a far cry from the hotdishes of my youth—elegant—using ingredients I have never heard of or seen at the market.

I linger over the desserts. Especially the pies. The favorite pie of my childhood—the high golden meringue lemon pie—rivaled that of my mother's, the one which won the prize at the county fair.

Then I find myself picking lemons from my neighbor's lemon tree. With the sweet sour scent of lemon on my hands, I put aside the artfully designed new cookbook and take out a recipe card marked, "Lemon Pie." The dog-eared card is yellowed from age.

And in the upper right corner, in Mother's handwriting, I read, "Angela's favorite."

DANCE, ANYONE?

Singles meet and dance,
smoke-ringed pockets of artificiality
hang over the ballroom.
Balding men group near door and bar,
anxious to escape;
perfume hangs heavily over long tables
as self-conscious women wait
with artfully made up faces
barely concealing their apprehension.
A first timer nervously giggles,
fiddling with a blue glass ring.
Her awkward smile too bright,
metallic over well-brushed teeth.
Smiling, he leans toward her,
his voice barely discernible above the music.
"Dance?"

HAIR HASSLES

I had "straight as a stick" hair during the heyday of revered waves. Furthermore, taming my maverick cowlick proved to be a hopeless task.

Memories of Mother setting me on the kitchen stool to give me a soup bowl haircut are bittersweet. Notwithstanding the protective towel over my shoulders, fastened by an oversized safety pin, hair escaped down my neck and back. The itching intense, I, a natural born wiggler, wiggled even more. To calm me, Mother sang a lovely song about an Indian maiden, making up the words as she snipped.

Years later, she curled my hair, heating the curling iron in the kerosene lamp. The iron's charred wooden handles protruded, as deer antlers, over the top of the smoked chimney. Again, I found it impossible to keep my head still so my ears became blistered, their red tops peeking through my hair.

Every June, after I became fourteen, I had a permanent.

A huge machine with dangling electric cords heated the rods which were rolled in my hair. I fantasized lightning striking the machine; therefore, I never had a perm during a storm since electrocution was even a worse fate than living with straight hair.

I shampooed my hair with coal-tar soap and rainwater caught in a barrel outside the porch door. After a vinegar rinse to remove the tangles, I applied a green gooey waveset and looped strands of hair around my fingers, fastening them flat with bobby pins. When dry, I combed these pincurls into waves.

Cold wave perms replaced the gigantic machine about the time curlers were discovered. They ranged from giant mesh-enclosed brushes to miniature ones for short hair, and all the sizes in-between. The curlers coincided with "beehive" hairstyles created by backcombing a pile of hair on top of the head. Strong and coarse hair worked well in a beehive, whereas my hair resembled a bird's nest.

Therefore, I compensated with a wig. Every artificial hair in place but my own hair lay cramped and matted under the wig. I literally removed my "beehive" every night.

Straight hair has come into its own! I have forsaken perms and wear it longer. Ironically, I realize it is no longer "straight as a stick." But what stick is straight? It has several bends in it.

I'm lucky. I don't need a psychologist or a counselor. My hairdresser listens to me. Really and truly. She greets me with the warmest of smiles, puts a plastic bib around my shoulders and hands me fresh coffee.

"How's Angie today?"

ANOTHER LIFE TO LIVE

Monday
The awareness has hit me this morning. A stark awareness. Cancer. Colon cancer, the second leading cause of death from cancer in both genders. I weep. My pencil weeps.

I remember Sunday. I flood the stool with an issue of rectal blood. I trail blood on white carpet, bed, sheets and mattress. I wrap my thighs with towels.

I am whisked to Emergency—still dressed in the hot pink dress I wore to church. I am ashen and shaking from nerves. Both the doctor and the nurse are competent and kind. The bleedings stops spontaneously but I remain in the Emergency Room more than four hours.

"See your doctor in the morning."

I do.

"I want you to have a colonoscopy tomorrow. We must find the etiology of this bleeding."

Tuesday
I return to the hospital, this time to the same day surgery wing. The fibroscopic examination and removal of the three polyps goes smoothly. After awakening from "twilight sleep," I am given a picture of the ugly specimens.

The nurse comments, "This one must have been there a long time. It's huge and was deeply embedded."

I am chilled.

"Your doctor will call in a week with the results from the laboratory. Don't lift heavy objects or exercise for twenty-four hours."

In the evening, I phone my daughter-in-law who has coped with breast cancer with dignity and grace.

She understands my fear.

"I felt the same way the day after the removal of the lump in my breast."

She, too, had cried all day.

Wednesday

I continue weeping. Bill listens to me talk about my fears. I phone family and friends and receive comfort. My pen comforts me.

What a marvelous and unique sense of humor God has! I lectured to hundreds of student nurses about colon cancer. I instructed them to wear a colostomy bag for twenty-four hours with something "spillable and smellable." If they wrote a paper on their experiences, I credited them ten points on their final exam. I wore one with every class.

Will I spend my last days with colon cancer? Yes, God does have gallows humor.

This task of dying gets complicated. I will leave everyone I love. Looking ahead to eternal life, I anticipate a reunion with my son, husband, parents and a host of relatives and friends, in addition to meeting the great welcomer, the Christ.

I wish some things in my life could be eradicated. I pray for forgiveness. But I continue weeping.

Thursday

It is Thanksgiving Day and I feel hopeful. I read that two out of three Americans over the age of sixty have some type of growth or lesion in their colon.

I cook a dinner for eight and notice that I am talking

too much. When I talk about God's gallows humor, my guests are not amused. They say, "Be positive."

Friday

Prodded by family and friends, I phone the doctor's office. I know Friday is harried but I can't wait any longer for the test results.

"The polyps are benign."

Sheer joy! Bill, too, is thrilled. I phone my army of supporters. I thank God for my new lease on life and pray that I will use it wisely.

A WOMAN OF COLOR AND CLASS

I abhor racial jokes and racial epithets. Even more, I abhor innuendoes about race.

During the tumultuous sixties, I antagonized acquaintances and friends with my stand on civil rights.

"If one of your sons marries one of 'them', you'll change your mind."

One did. I didn't change my mind. Rather—it reinforced my convictions.

An early fall evening, Mike and I stood in front of the fireplace with the Norwegian Coat of Arms on a large tapestry hanging over the mantle, a prized possession signifying my proud ancestry.

"What are you busy doing, Mike?"

"I'm dating and she happens to be black."

Deb came with Mike on his next visit. I opened the door to see a tall and regal black woman standing beside my son. The three of us sat in the living room and within minutes her personality captivated me.

Soon after, they married. Both returned to college. He graduated in vocational rehabilitation therapy, she in nursing.

After years of nursing in cardiac intensive care, Deb changed careers. She presently manages a restaurant in a facility sponsored by national, state and local funds for homeless people with disabilities who are in treatment. Open to the public, the Full Circle Cafe has established a reputation for culinary excellence.

The cafe is also a center for the arts. Each month, Deb sponsors an artist and the walls are hung with paintings. An evening with the artist is accompanied by local musicians. There are book readings and signings by regional authors. A monthly dinner featuring the "Chef of the Month" has capacity seating.

Deb sings, accompanied by Mike, with a local band.

Their mixed race marriage of over twenty years endures. Two handsome bi-racial children, a boy and girl, are now adults.

Mike and Deb enjoy an expanding circle of friends. In crisis, I confide in my daughter-in-law and am consoled by long distance counseling.

She is my friend, this woman of color and class.

THE GULF WAR

Too young to grasp the agony
    of World War II,
too busy to comprehend the
    wretchedness of Viet Nam,
this Gulf Conflict thrusts itself upon me,
the calculated horror of it all,
armchair authorities
    prophesy Armagedon.
My mind is saturated with war news.
Yet, I demand more,
switching TV channels
to hear the ghastly sound of missiles
and watch them light the sky
as if celebrating a gigantic, horrific
Fourth of July.

A STOLE WITH CLASS

Stoles were the fad of the day. Worn in lieu of a jacket, these long and beautiful scarves matched or contrasted with dresses. Mother crocheted a stole for me. A stole with class, out of white and gold metallic thread.

I planned to wear this classy creation for the first time at the social event of the season, my cousin Beverly's wedding.

Mother had a different idea.

"Angela, you have several nice things to wear so I told Grandma she could wear your stole to the wedding."

She added, "Unless, of course, you mind."

Mind? I had, in my imagination, worn it with aplomb to the wedding. I said nothing. True, I had the rest of my life to wear the stole and Grandma was over eighty.

Grandma proudly walked down the aisle in my new stole.

As in a fairy tale, the wedding was beautiful. The bride radiant. The groom tall, dark and handsome. The bride's sisters sang a duet and Ed, waiting at the altar, listened to Beverly sing, "Through the years I'll take my place beside you . . ." Superb music.

But my heart didn't sing. All I could think about was the stole. However, I wore it to many other events before it rested more than a decade in the trunk until I draped it over a table.

A table which needed a stole with class.

WINDPOWER

I awaken to hear the wind whistling near my front step, catching the windchimes in a wind wakeup call.

Sleepily, I wonder when does a breeze become a wind? That gentle childlike breeze which grows in intensity until it becomes an adult gale.

The wind has created a whimsical snow sculpture by my front door. Its swirls become a memorial to winter.

I turn on the radio to hear a blizzard has invaded even as I slept. School cancellations abound. St. Luke's School of Nursing is closed for the day.

The phone rings. It is another nursing instructor.

"No school today."

I, a link in the communication chain, phone another faculty member with the same message.

I tap off the alarm and curl into my bed, snug and content, for a long winter's nap.

THE RUNAWAY

I'm mad at Mama. Real mad. She scolded me for chasing kitty. She doesn't love me anymore so I am going to run away from home.

I pack my Sunday dress and shoes into my red wagon. My dog, Patsey, at my side, I walk real fast down the long driveway, so fast the wagon hits me on the back of my foot.

My three girl cousins live on neighboring farms. I turn in the direction of their homes. I know either of my two aunts would love to have another five-year-old little girl, even if my mama doesn't want me. Tears wash my cheeks. They taste salty, like Daddy's popcorn.

The hill is high and my red wagon pulls hard in the gravel. A car passes and both the red wagon and I are covered with dust.

Another hill is even higher. I already miss my mama; maybe I shouldn't have chased kitty.

After the next big hill, I decide to turn around and go home. Patsey runs ahead of me. I notice that for both of us, going home goes faster than leaving home.

At the end of our driveway, kitty at her feet, Mama is waiting for me.

I pick up my little brown and white kitten and start to cry.

"I'm sorry, Mama."

She puts her arms around me, kisses me and says, "Don't run away, darling, you're my little girl and I love you."

I never ran away from home again.

DESTRUCTION

A shining space shuttle appealed
    to our imagination,
mirrored on TV.
We gasped as ice crystallized
    the human cargo
exploding before the eyes
    of the nation.
A staggering conical swirl
    of destruction
heading nowhere.

FEET

I am the not-so-proud owner of the largest feet in our family. Mother had, the salesman said, a perfect foot, small and narrow with beautiful toes. (I added the beautiful toe bit). My sister, Marie, also has a Cinderella foot.

Perhaps I am ahead of my time because I notice most young women of today have larger feet than their mothers. These young women don't appear to worry about their feet. They proudly wear sandals and walking shoes which rival Paul Bunyan of Minnesota folklore. (Sorry, Mrs. Paul Bunyan).

Indeed, this makes me wonder if the ugly red protrusions which extend next to the great toe are named after Paul or was it an accidental pairing of names.

Perhaps because I didn't inherit the beautiful feet, I adore beautiful shoes. Platforms and pumps, stiletto heels and sandals cluster in my closet. Many are older and out-of-date; however, if one lives a long life everything comes full circle. I may dust those stiletto heels and see where they will take me.

Probably to the emergency room.

EXCUSES

I've vowed never to look at the back of my closet or bathroom doors again. On both doors are taped sheets of exercises.

These exercises are guaranteed to flatten my abdomen and trim my hips in just six weeks. Miracle exercises.

It's amazing how six weeks come and go without my starting to exercise. I stay awake nights inventing reasons not to get started.

The slim creatures pictured look as I looked at eight years of age. Sticks. The contortions assumed by these unbelievable figures are strange.

To salve my conscience and for fun, I ride my trusty one-speed bike. However, I keep the posters on the doors, shades of what might be or might have been.

REFLECTIONS

However and whenever you look into them, mirrors are both an abomination and a blessing.

A mirror reflects careful grooming with gorgeous clothes and an exquisite coiffure. A mirror reflects figure flaws, unkempt hair and a crooked hemline. It may reflect a horrific touch of white slipping below that crooked hemline.

A mirror reflects the happiness of a bride, the pride of a groom, the joy of new parents and a baby's first smile. Mirrors reflect the love and turmoil of a family.

A mirror may be simple, a mere reflecting glass or ornate with beveled edges and a wide carved frame.

The utilitarian mirror of a compact enables quick makeup repair. A mirrored tray enhances small treasures.

Mirrors are a designer's delight. They bring light into a dark room, creating windows where there are none, thus doubling the size of the room.

Mirrors reflect spring greens and the reds and golds of fall, fading into winter white.

Truly a mirror is indispensable. It reflects who and where we are.

OF SPUN GOLD

In the dawn's gray light, a gigantic tractor guided the steel threshing machine which resembled a giant giant caterpillar—its mighty arms swaying in the breeze—as it rumbled up our driveway.

"The threshers are here," Mother said, drying her hands on her apron.

She was ready for them. In our front yard were four sawhorses topped by a huge sheet of plywood; an improvised table large enough to seat more than a dozen men.

Her small kitchen was steamy. Up since 5 a.m., she had baked four lemon pies, their meringue hats high and handsome, which were cooling on the table. The day before I helped her peel, it seemed, tons of potatoes. Both a roast ready for the oven and a pail of peas to be shelled waited nearby.

I ran outdoors to watch the activity. During the next hour, six hayracks powered by two horses apiece, arrived. The hayracks creaked on large wagon wheels. The workhorses were well-fed and groomed, their coats shining in the early morning sun.

The hayrack drivers were well fed too! Most gained weight during threshing because of the humongous meals provided by the farmers' wives.

There were two men to a hayrack, usually a farmer and his teen-age son. They drove to a field covered with golden shocks of wheat. Returning with a full load, both were perched high atop the bundles in the hayrack.

Soon the activity accelerated. The top heavy wagons lined up in front of the giant beast and men threw bundles into its gaping jaws. As if by magic, the grain came out one arm and the chaff blew out the other. Slowly, the straw stack of spun gold grew. My arms and legs and especially my neck, damp from the humidity of the August day, itched from the chaff which escaped into the farmyard.

An open truck with high boarded sides stood ready to haul the grain to an elevator fifteen miles away.

Later, the handsome young men and their fathers gathered around the makeshift table. I delighted in serving them; keeping the bowls of mashed potatoes, gravy, peas, as well as the platters of roast beef, filled. Later, I served the lemon pie with the sheer egg coffee. Although cognizant of the young men, I shyly averted my eyes while serving them.

Soon the two days of threshing were over and the huge beast lumbered down our driveway. My father stacked the sawhorses and plywood table top into the granary in readiness for the next year's threshers.

Our household again reduced to Mother, Dad, my younger sister Marie and me, only the memories of the frenetic activity during the threshing days remained. However, money generated from the crop came just in time to buy new shoes for school.

ANOTHER MIRACLE

Something happens each Christmas
I can't set my watch
when it will happen
but all of a sudden Christmas is here
in my heart,
in my very being.
The Holy Spirit takes over,
it is indeed another miracle.
Gifts or no gifts,
He comes,
with the promise of everlasting love,
salvation, and all of life to come.
For Christmas is the threshold
of eternal life,
and Christ is the great welcomer.

DISHWASHING

Half of each year I wash dishes. The other half? A robot takes over. The dishwasher.

Therefore, I am in a unique position to evaluate the two methods of cleaning dishes. Both have merit.

In my Arizona home, the dishwasher dominates the kitchen. It washes a full load effortlessly. Dishes and silver gleam. I am free to clean counters, table and sink as it works. But it needs special dishwasher soap.

Dishwashing soap leads to chaos. My husband discovered this, to his chagrin.

However, dishwashing is a lonely task. A dishwasher doesn't talk and I have not begun to talk to it. Perhaps that time will come.

At my lake cottage in Minnesota, I dominate the kitchen. Angela, the dishwasher. Sometimes my husband and friends join me.

The dish towels in Minnesota are used. Worn. But the glasses sparkle, as do the old mismatched plates. I wash as fast as I can for the water is hot. Very hot.

What a timeless task—washing and drying dishes. However, confidences are shared in the quiet of the kitchen among the pots and pans. Stories abound. Successes and failures are shared as well as aspirations and anguish. Over that most humble of housekeeping tasks, washing dishes, there is laughter and tears.

I notice the diamond on the third finger of my left hand shines brightly following its immersion in the suds in the sink. But my hands thirst for lotion.

Drying dishes, a guest makes a contribution to the dinner. Whereas in my modern kitchen, the guest is unnecessary so we sit and chat in another room. That's good, too.

Therefore, I enjoy both methods of cleaning dishes and it prevents boredom.

ACCIDENT PRONE

"What happened to Angela now?" our neighbor, Clara, asked Mother on the telephone.

From the wisdom of years, I understand the validity of the question. I was an accident prone child. Ours was a party line and phone calls were subject to a "rubber necker's" interpretation.

My accidents provided grist for the gossips. Like the time I bounded down the porch steps and fell on the sharp wooden stakes my father had placed in the petunia bed to discourage our dog, Patsey, from lying in it.

This puncture wound refused to heal. It festered. Mother's hot packs of no avail. Finally, the doctor drained the pus from the wound and kept probing until he discovered the small head of the stake, wedged between the tibia and fibula.

My blood flowed freely during the procedure. Dad fainted at the sight of his daughter's blood. Too traumatic.

The granulation tissue on my right forearm attests to yet another accident when I attempted to run through a barb wire fence. Mother poured peroxide and bandaged it. This time—no infection. Only an unsightly scar.

I've fallen from the hay loft and the roof of our house without breaking a bone. I've sprained a ligament and wore a dishtowel sling for six weeks after being bucked off my horse, Jerry. The ice on the skating rink shattered when I acquired an embarrassing black eye. Forty years later, a friend informed me the ice on the rink was still shattered! Because I always ran, I endured scraped knees and ripped skirts.

Now, an older, wiser adult, I've become cautious. I watch where I run.

SEIZE THE MOMENT TO:

Thank God for a wonderful sleep
and a beautiful morning

Send that birthday card
and that sympathy note

Water those plants
Spot the rug

Clean those drawers
Scrub that floor

Wash the dishes
Polish those windows

Cherish your friends
Love your enemies.

Tonight, pray for a better tomorrow
for all God's children.

IS BIGGER BETTER?

In America, bigger is better. It is a national preoccupation.

Last week we replaced our eighteen-year-old mattress with a new one twice its height. It visually fills the room.

"If we fall out of this, it will be a high fall."

"You'll just have to wear a parachute."

Truly, under the concept "bigger is better," the sky is the limit.

Housing, for example. Many new subdivisions boast houses which take three maids to keep clean; huge and vacant mansions with both occupants stressfully employed.

Many are employed by giant conglomerates with corporate offices in most states. The home office building is located in the largest city in our nation where its tower grazes the sky.

People are growing too, both taller and wider. Scales weigh at higher levels and bathtubs resemble huge swimming pools. With jets.

Therefore, clothes come larger under the same size. My husband bought a large size shirt. Only the neck fit and he was lost in a polyester tent.

Jumbo jets fly hundreds of passengers. In the new millennium, we may expect two tier London bus seating on planes.

To accommodate the larger appetites, restaurant

meals are so large they require additional plates on which to heap the food.

Even house parties are bigger. They are no longer cozy dinners for four or six but sixty to a hundred guests are invited. These guests are served by uniformed caterers.

Home theaters abound with huge screens and oversized seats; the rooms are large enough to accommodate a small army.

The same houses sport libraries where oversized books crowd deep shelves.

However, prisons are larger and police officers have quadrupled.

Cities are growing and suburbs are connected by six-lane highways.

Even retirement villages are larger and more elaborate. Most are built around golf courses and large country clubs.

However, a dramatic mattress doesn't guarantee sleep. Overfed people aren't guaranteed longer lives. Larger homes don't guarantee happier marriages. Larger cities don't guarantee more productive lives.

Is bigger better?

FORGING FRIENDSHIPS

"Mother, Dari doesn't like me," the little girl sobbed.

This little girl grew up. She graduated from college and later immersed herself in marriage, children and career.

But every once in a while, she "knew" a colleague or an acquaintance "didn't like her."

Did she like that person? The answer, an unequivocal, "No."

Most of us meet dozens of new people each year. We meet them on the golf course, at church or parties and other social events.

What vibes do we send out? Is our body language open—leaning forward to listen with good eye contact? Or are we closed, arms hugging our chest, our restless eyes searching the room as the other is talking?

Only a minority of our acquaintances become friends. Only a tiny fraction of friends become close friends. Indispensable friends. Less than ten. For friends of the heart are hard to find; the intellectual and emotional join to create an interpersonal relationship which is mutually accepting, bonded by shared commonalties.

Little girl, now an adult, how you are seen by others is but a reflection of how you see them. Or see yourself.

REMEMBRANCES OF CHRISTMAS PAST

You remember the skates you didn't get when you were ten. The year there were no gifts and no tree.

You remember when the brown bag given to you after the church program broke from the weight of the apple. Your red and green ribbon candy shattered and later ground into colored powder on the basement stairs.

You remember never being an angel in the Christmas pageant. Always a narrator. A narrator who wanted to be an angel. A narrator who sat full of anxiety in the front pew before reading, "And it came to pass in those days . . ."

You remember your father's death two days after Christmas and these many years later, tears sting your eyelids.

You remember the Christmas your son was hospitalized; you, his mother, helpless.

You pause, reflecting on all these things until you are overwhelmed by the wondrous Christmases of other years.

You remember the fun and laughter shared over your mother's holiday dinner table, a table resplendent with the linen and newly polished silver.

You remember your father telling a story of anticipating a Christmas goose dinner while in the trenches during World War II. He received, he said with great drama, "the tip of the wing."

You remember meeting your cousins at the "Big Hill"

during Christmas vacation where, after making angels in the snow, you skied until dark.

You remember wearing a red velvet dress with a green silk sash, handmade by your mother. This, a Christmas when you were a confident narrator.

You remember when, years later, your sons sang at their church program.

You remember, with a smile, your tone deaf son proudly pulling the curtain at his Christmas school cantata.

You remember your sons and their friends crowded into the breakfast nook, frosting Christmas cookies, their mouths ringed with red and green.

You remember those sons presenting a Christmas Eve program following the traditional lefse and lutefisk supper. The lutefisk about which they complained but devoured every morsel on the platter.

You remember the time they presented such a long program of recitations, piano solos and duets, that your mother said, "Isn't it time to open the presents?"

You reflect on all these things as you and your husband sit alone by the tree on Christmas Eve. Slowly, he opens the Bible to read those magical words, bright with joy and promise, "And it came to pass in those days . . ."

VACATION, A REDEDICATION TO LIFE

A vacation is a respite from your ordinary run-of-the-mill life.

There are two types of vacations, the "stay-at-home and paint the house" kind of vacation or the "see the world in two weeks" kind of vacation. Both have merit. Both can be deadly.

You plan your vacation months in advance. The remodeling project awaits your skill with tools and your paint brush awaits the cash flow to finish the job. You spend ordinary evenings planning your extraordinary projects.

You are down to your last detail and your last cent when vacation finally arrives. The temptation to sleep until noon is too tempting to resist and you anxiously consult your calendar.

Your paint and face lift operation on your home comes to fruition. Each day you survey your work and clean off a small spot on the table for dinner. You order in pizza. By the time your two-week vacation is over, you never want another bite of pizza. However, your house looks lovely in its new gown and you are ready for your rest—to return to work.

Thinking ahead to your "see the world" vacation, you avidly read the folders obtained from the travel agency. The multi-colored pictures of far away, exotic places, inhabited by friendly folks eager to cater to your every whim, overwhelms you. You spend long hours thinking of these wondrous places to visit or perhaps move to.

Finally, you put your travel folders aside and board a plane embarking for Europe. A trip of a lifetime. Your travel guide is fantastic and knows every geographical detail of the country as well as dozens of shops. The food in every hotel is exquisite. Most hotels are owned by wealthy Americans. The mattresses are firm, the rooms are quiet. You sleep 3,000 miles from home as if in your own bed.

But you never have a conversation with the inhabitants of any countries you visit. You don't share tea or coffee with any family. Nor do you tour a school, a hospital or a factory. You meet dozens of Americans everywhere. Like you.

You may plan to rent a lake cabin in the pines for a week next July. When the week arrives, it rains every day except the morning you leave for home.

If you have renovated your home during vacation, you have enjoyed a change of pace and gained a fine feeling of self-worth with your accomplishment.

Whereas, if you tour the world or spend time at a lake cottage, you find that the grass truly is greener and your home decor brighter than you remember.

You remove your shoes and stretch.

"It's good to be home."

That's what a vacation is all about—a rededication to ordinary living.

FAITH

Please Lord, take my
    mustard seed of faith
Help me fertilize it with prayer
And water it by tears
Make it grow by your love
Into a strong and healthy shade tree.

EYES

Eyes upstage names. Everytime. One becomes engrossed in observing a stranger's blue, brown or green eyes, only half hearing the name.

An acquaintance with glassy eyes may appear to look at you without seeing you. Others, with friendly, folksy eyes may visit yours for a long moment. Eye contact.

You notice some eyes are happy while others are sad and wonder . . .

Some glasses draw attention to themselves rather than the eye. Some rims convey the color of the iris—others complement it—a wearer's choice. Rimless glasses are a window dressing for the eye.

Contacts make for clearer vision if they are wearer friendly. They may be color matched for any eye.

Eyes reflect the vacant stare of a person affected with dementia. Whereas, the eyes of a newborn are unquestionably beautiful but one also questions how much they, too, can comprehend.

The dressed up, go-to-party eyes with lashes blackened by mascara and lids overwhelmed by deep and colorful shadow sometimes ages a woman.

A student's eyes are red rimmed from lack of sleep before an exam. Blind eyes may depend on a cane, a friend, or a seeing eye dog for their vision. Lovers have eyes which embrace.

Surgeries such as eyelifts and removal of fatty, under-the-eye deposits (bags) improve one's appearance.

You wonder when the eyes of a sweet and inquisitive child change to the hooded but intense glare of the thief, the rapist or the plunderer.

Truly, the eyes are windows of the soul.

MAD HENS

Its inhabitants dangerous for invaders, our chicken coop became a miniature war zone.

Two sides of this rectangular building were covered by wall to wall cubicles resembling post office boxes, only larger. They were straw-filled cubicles, comfortable nests for the hens to lay their eggs.

These hens were territorial and tyrannical. They guarded their eggs as a lioness guards her cubs. I was "scared stiff" by these hens and they knew it. Every time I picked eggs, I was pecked. A hen seized my skin whenever she became frightened or angry. One mad hen flew to my shoulder and pecked my earlobe.

That was the last time I picked eggs. I bargained with Mother. If I washed dishes, she would pick eggs.

Dressed for a war zone in Dad's red wool plaid jacket and striped overalls rolled high so she could walk, this pretty little mother of mine became a sight to behold—barely recognizable.

She had a winning way with the hens. They never even thought of plucking out her eyes as they had planned to do to me. They never even thought of holding her hostage as they had planned for me. They never even thought of an all-out attack on her as they had planned for me.

No, each sat calmly on her nest and laid her daily egg.

COPPER BOILERS

It, like the rest of us, is beautiful in retirement. The hundred-year-old copper boiler, green from patina, is now full of trailing blue verbena.

It, like the rest of us, deserves its retirement. An authentic hard-working, honest-to-goodness boiler tended lovingly on the kitchen range by my grandma. Her face was pink from stirring the swirling suds with her stick, made from a cut-off broom handle.

Sometimes the clothes needed a gentle rub on the washboard to remove a spot the boiler missed.

The boiler rests on my patio floor. A conversation piece. It seems all grandmothers had copper boilers and wood ranges.

THE REUNION

It is your 50th high school reunion. Unbelievable. You wish you could look beautiful. Or semi-beautiful. Even attractive.

In two months you must accomplish the impossible. You diet. You starve. You eat ten pounds of carrot sticks and sixteen heads of lettuce. Nothing else. But the scale doesn't budge.

You shop for a new outfit. The stunning ones are in size four or six. Finally, you find *the* dress. You like what you see in the mirror. Black slims. If the dressmaker eases the fabric over the hips, it will fit fine.

Because black brings out the shadows under your eyes, you experiment with a cover-up makeup. It's too late for plastic surgery.

You find a lovely multi-colored scarf for the neck. A pearl pin holds it securely. The pearl earrings you received on your tenth wedding anniversary and the black heels you wore last month at your daughter's wedding both work well.

Finally, the day arrives. Your hairdresser tames and tints your hair. You keep your husband waiting a half-hour while you apply your makeup.

The dinner is delightful; however, you notice your classmates are as starved as you are. Downright hungry. Old nostalgic pictures are passed around the table but most are busy eating.

You notice your classmates all look fifty years older—

even the cheerleaders look matronly.

You are surprised when your best friend in high school doesn't recognize you.

Perhaps you have become beautiful in fifty years.

Or in two months.

MY ROSE GARDEN

The roses in my garden
are getting thorny, Lord.
They are replaced by cacti,
bristling state-of-the-art cacti.
No amount of watering helps.
The weeds in my garden
    are growing, Lord.
Thriving from neglect.
Little pockets of fear grow
    among my prayers.
Keep my rose of faith healthy, Lord.
Water it with trust,
fertilize it with patience.
Bend its petals toward
    the sunshine of your love.
Remind me, Lord, to
    thank you for my garden.

COMPUTERS AND ME

Computer illiterate, not I. I've joined a beginning computer class in readiness for the 21st century. I've committed to 12 hour-long lessons.

The instructor asks us to introduce ourselves.

"I don't own a computer and the only class I ever dropped was typing."

"You just warm my heart by telling me that," she retorts with a smile.

"Why are you taking the class?"

"I write a newspaper column and it would be easier for the editor to read my copy."

Computerese—a vocabulary all its own. I wonder if it is in the dictionary. A new dictionary. It brings to mind, are dictionaries, as computers, obsolete as soon as you buy them?

I try to concentrate in class. I try hard.

At 7 a.m. I start having trouble; by 8 o'clock, I am in deep trouble.

It took three classes before I felt comfortable turning on the computer. Another two classes before I could maneuver the mouse. I can see why it's named mouse, all mice are hard to control.

One look at the word, menu, and I am reminded I haven't had breakfast.

I notice that I am the only honest-to-goodness beginner in the Beginning Computer class. Just like in the typing class years ago.

But this time I won't quit.

IF YOU . . .

Stub your toe on the way to the kitchen,
worse yet, fracture that toe.

Run out of milk for breakfast,
and bread for toast.

Find your cereal soggy
and ants in the sugar bowl.

You may as well go back to bed.

EARRINGS

"Sally, if you start wearing those silly earrings, soon there will only be one."

My dad was stern in his admonition to my mother. Dogmatic.

Undaunted, it spurred my spirited mother to buy a pair of exquisite, if tiny, pearl earrings. She wore them every day. By the time I was the age to consider wearing earrings, Dad was conditioned to the idea and Mother was all for it.

I expect that is the reason I can't throw earrings away—even when there is only one. Sooner or later, I may find its mate under a cushion or behind the furniture. Sometimes I do.

Therefore, I have a drawer full of earrings from all the stages of my life. There are checkbook boxes full of junk jewelry in brilliant colors. There are the tiny pierced and the larger clamp-on earrings. Diamond studs and miniature opal teardrops look as new.

I wear each once a year, sometimes less. But in each piece lies a bit of history. My history.

There are even a few sets of earrings and necklaces, such as a brilliant necklace of iridescent colors set in black with matching earrings and lapel pin. Over fifty years they have rested in my drawer until last Christmas I wore them with a black formal. They looked new, as brilliant as ever. I felt young wearing them, although they, as I, qualify as antiques.

Someday I'll empty that jewelry drawer and toss those time-worn earrings. But the right occasion and right dress may come along and I'll wish I still had them.

My sister or my husband give me beautiful earrings for birthday and Christmas. They soon join my other favorites in the drawer. Gathering history.

I may divide my earrings between my granddaughters, Morgan, Nicole and Kayla, to start their own collection.

Then again, parting with old friends is difficult.

AFTER THE DANCE

Candace realized suddenly that she had promised two fellas the first dance at the get-acquainted dance at the college.

As the music started, she recognized a friend from home.

"Brian, please sit out a dance with two boys and myself. I really need your help because I can't dance with both of them at the same time."

"My pleasure. I'm a little too nervous to ask a strange girl to dance, anyway."

Both Dean and Tom came to dance with her.

"Do you mind if we all just sit this one out? I did a silly thing by promising the first dance with both of you."

She hoped she smiled convincingly.

Brian led the others to a quiet corner behind the artificial palms, far away from the orchestra.

How they talked! Dean, a pre-seminary student, the quietest; whereas Ned, the most talkative, planned a business career with his father after graduation.

"That is, if I graduate," he said ruefully. "I'm already scared of the place. I got lost today trying to find the cafeteria and ended up in the science hall."

Brian injected, "I'm scared, too. That professor of advanced algebra—seems he is out to get us all out of here—and soon."

"Oh, you have Mr. Johnson the third hour? So do I. Isn't he dreadful? Where do you sit? I hadn't notice you before," Candace said.

"Close to the window so I can stay awake. It's warm and I get drowsy listening to him drone on in his monotone."

Candace was surprised to hear Brian because he was an A student in high school.

She took notice of his friendly, round face and lovely manners. She really hadn't known him well in high school as there were over 700 in her class. She knew him more by reputation.

During intermission they were still talking. Brian asked her to dance and the other two boys excused themselves and asked other girls to dance.

She thought, *He can dance well, too*, and felt relaxed with him. Comfortable.

"May I walk you to your dorm?"

The answer was "Yes."

Eleven years later, Candace remembered the dance as she walked into her sunny kitchen and started breakfast for Brian and their three sons.

If she hadn't promised to dance with two men at the same time, she may not have had these little boy treasures, let alone the love of her life.

RAPPORT

We meet,
instant recognition
of another's soul.

FINGERNAILS

When a child, I saw a movie by a missionary to China. One of the Chinese men was purported to be wealthy as demonstrated by his long fingernails. Memory tells me they were so long they touched his feet but memory tends to hyperbolize.

These were not the fingernails for piano playing or milking cows, I thought, looking down at my short, clipped nails.

My nails still are short and functional, a pale pink in color.

A part of me has always yearned for nails of glitter and glamour, red nails, blue nails, green nails, designer nails; but life decreed otherwise. I had and have a working woman's nails.

A friend has nails so long and strong, it takes hours to groom them. They look beautiful polished and she moves her hands expressively as she talks.

They look just like mine in my dreams.

ONE WOMAN'S HANDS

A woman's hands change over the years
from the constantly moving hands of a
baby with pink palms
    and dimpled knuckles,
to the smooth hands of a teenager,
her future unknown.

The busy hands of a career
    woman and mother
become, with time, the
    wrinkled, sometimes
arthritic hands of a grandmother.
Each of these hands are folded in prayer.

PLAGUED BY PERFECTIONISM

Are you afflicted by the plague of perfectionism? Go ahead, deny it. All perfectionists do. They tell the rest of us slobs, "If a job is worth doing, it's worth doing well."

The trouble is that they keep doing a job over and over, so hung up on minute details that the job never gets done.

In writing, perfectionists rewrite and polish, then repolish until they tire of their task. A housewife dusts and sweeps until her dustcloth is full of holes and her broom is worn to nubbins. A working woman drives a spotless car. She has every hair in place with nary a hangnail.

Bathrooms gleam with just the right accents and matching soap. Furniture is precisely arranged.

Perfectionists expect their husbands, friends, even acquaintances to be perfect, too. Their reaction?

"But I can't do it as well as you," and they don't attempt to do so.

Pity the child who muddies the kitchen floor with his boots. Pity the husband who drapes his bathrobe over the bedroom chair and tosses his sweaty socks in a corner.

Strange, most perfectionists seem to be women. How many dustballs are under your bed?

RAINY DAY BLESSINGS

It's raining. The sound on the roof comforts me. There is no need to venture out so I relax in my chair and listen to the dancing raindrops on my windowpane.

I think of all the blessings of rain, especially gentle rain like this. A blessed boon for farmers, their fields thirsting for drink; the plants only pacified by irrigation. Soon the fields will grow and even the desert will bloom.

Somehow my home is cozier, a day made for reading. A day made for creating nature on canvas with my paintbrush. Well-watered landscapes. I harbor no guilt writing letters or sitting hours just wiling away time because I am immersed in a cocoon, not of my own choosing.

Today small children will splash in rain puddles to see how high the water will fly. I expect they feel big and strong, knowing they can make their way in the world, as a big splash on a rainy day.

Our daily paper, encased in plastic, lies under the eaves of the garage. It invites me to read it more carefully than usual. Ah, the benefits of a rainy day.

Remembrances of raindrops falling on the kitchen windows in the farmhouse of my childhood seem as yesterday. Dad played Monopoly with me because it was too wet to go to the fields. He always won. Well, nearly always. We played for hours, our only interruptions were noon dinner, afternoon lunch and supper.

Mother busied herself with cookie and bread baking

on rainy days and those wonderful aromas permeated our little house. Dad and I ate the crumbles, the cookie misfits, even as we parked in a hotel on Boardwalk or Park Place.

Later, I remember rainy days with my four sons. The living room was a gymnasium where they romped, wrestled and watched "Howdy Doody" and "The Three Stooges." Some rainy days, they too, played Monopoly.

True to my training, I baked cookies and bread on rainy days. True to their heritage, they ate the cookie crumbles. Even worse, they ate the cookies as fast as they came from the oven and created crumbles. Four cookies per boy equaled sixteen cookies. Half a batch of chocolate chip cookies.

These many years later, the frustration of having cookies disappear too fast has dimmed. But the joy of hearing my sons' laughter lingers.

I think of my newly planted petunias and imagine how beautiful they will look tomorrow. Dewy fresh.

I think of the four newly planted trees in our backyard and rejoice that they are well watered.

The rain over, I watch a robin searching for worms to fill her fat, red belly. I notice the water is higher on the dock and next door the three-year-old is splashing in the puddles.

Then, I bow my head to thank God for the rain which renews all things and gives one pause to rest and think.

RAIN

It rained last night,
slow, deep, penetrating rain.
I was glad to be inside
covered, warm and safe.

This morning the air is fresh.
Trees lift their leaves.
Grasses tingle with delight,
as they and I greet another day.

THE COUNTY FAIR

The county fair is in town! You polish your bike fenders with furniture polish and whiten your sidewall tires with shoe polish before you bike the fifteen miles to town to go to the fair with your cousin.

When the county fair is in town, everyone and everything changes. A town's quiet streets are full of people. Boisterous people.

Cars whiz up and down main street and eventually end up parked in or near the fairgrounds.

The Midway dominates the scene. Colorful cotton candy is everywhere. Popcorn stands abound. Music grinds from the merry-go-round, Ferris wheels scrape the sky. Novelty rides, each more frightening than the next, spill change from your pocket and fear from your heart.

Hoarse-voiced men invite you to toss a ring around a peg to win the prize, usually a doll or stuffed toy. Hundreds of lights blink and beckon you to sideshows of dubious worth. Even the air is electric.

In the beer gardens, the beer flows, foaming freely from the top.

Nearby are the church food stands. One sits on plank seating and watches the women working. They serve potato salad and beans, hamburgers and hotdogs with splendid apple, cheery and pumpkin pies, made from scratch.

Located far from the food stands are the barns. Beautifully groomed horses are tended by their proud owners. Carefully curried cattle are exhibited. There are white, red, blue and best of show ribbons prominently displayed. The barns are warm with the heat from the animals; pungent odors waft in the night air and flies are everywhere.

The 4-H barns appear to be the favorite. They are crowded with teen-age girls. Their brothers and friends show off their prize animals. One notices many girls spend more time looking at the boy than at his animal.

The pavilion with garden produce is impressive with large and lovely fruits and vegetables. One of its rooms showcase perfectly canned vegetables and tables with beautifully baked pastries. Many are tagged with ribbons of excellence. Young 4-H girls have baked breads, cakes and cookies. One wonders how the judges can decide the winner because all seem winners.

The air is humid. A thunderstorm is imminent; people scatter to shelter to wait out the shower.

The grandstand comes alive in the evening. A 4-H style queen is crowned, wearing her self-styled dress.

Afterward, an act is on stage, the best the Fair Board can offer with limited money and limited seating. Local musicians add dash before they introduce the "special" act. This act may be aerialists flying from trapeze to trapeze, then bowing to the audience in their showy stage costumes.

Later, at home, you practice the aerialist act, flying through the air on your parents' mattress. The bed breaks under your bouncing.

You decide the fair was worth spending those dimes, nickels and pennies you faithfully saved in the green Ball fruit jar.

WHITE ORGANDY DRESSES

by Marie Erickson Saterbak

Celia rushed about the large kitchen with a sense of urgency, her ankle-length, gray poplin skirt swirling around her as she turned, revealing shapely legs above high-buttoned shoes. Her thick brown hair struggled as if trapped by its heavy braids, criss-crossed at her neck.

She lit a match on the side of the cook stove, hoping it would catch into flames quickly, and turned to the cistern hand pump to get the water for the day. Usually it took twenty pumps and a prime of water for success. Today Celia was weary and everything seemed more difficult.

A crib crowded the corner of the room. Herbran had moved it there his morning so she could better watch Mabel. Celia placed a small hand on the crib and observed her child anxiously. Now, finally in sleep, Mabel breathed heavily, her face flushed with unnatural rosiness; her five-year-old, thin legs too long for the crib, pushing out between the chipped metal rails. Four-year-old Alma pulled at her skirt.

"Mama, my neck hurts," complained Alma.

Celia tried desperately to hang on to her patience. She felt tired to her bones. Any minute now Herbran and the hired man would be in from the barn, wanting breakfast.

Her neck. What a strange thing to say, thought Celia. *Oh, no! She means her throat, I suppose. Children are forever calling things by the wrong name. That means she's got it, too. I know she's got it. Both my babies. Both my little girls.*

"Lie down a while, Alma. I'll get you some hot rhubarb juice. It feels good on sore throats."

The doctor had been to the house two days ago. Celia remembered his horses making noises outside the house and was acutely aware of her jealousy.

Herbran's horse had broken its leg last fall and had needed to be shot. Now Herbran had to walk everywhere, even thirty miles to the mill to have the wheat ground into flour. He had walked the thirteen miles to town to talk to the doctor. Now Celia felt invaded by this strange man in her house—even in the children's room.

"How long has she been sick?" he asked.

"Three days. She can't eat. It hurts her to swallow."

Celia's oval blue eyes were brimming as if to spill little blue beads down her pale, well-chiseled face.

"It's a mean sickness. Diphtheria. Catchy, too. You better watch the other one. They get this fever and this stuff in their throat. Can't seem to cough it up. Can't eat. Even hard to swallow. The whole countryside is plagued."

He went on, but Celia had heard no more than the dreaded word, diphtheria. Their neighbors, one homestead away, had buried their three-year-old son only two weeks ago.

She remembered with a funny little squeeze in her chest how beautiful her Mabel and Alma had looked the day of little Jeb's funeral. It was a sad occasion but there had been so many people milling about, eating and eventually even laughing, that she kept thinking it was almost like a party.

She also remembered how smug she had felt. Her two daughters in their new white organdy dresses— every seam perfect. Celia sewed painstakingly well—a tribute to her mother, who did dressmaking yet in Norway.

And Herbran. Yes, Herbran was truly the best of all the husbands. Tall, with blondish-brown hair, combed back from a tanned honest brow with its deep-set greenish-blue eyes. It was his eyes she had first noticed when she met Herbran at the township picnic. They were so direct. Like Herbran himself. Always kind, sometimes abrupt, he pragmatically did what he needed to do.

"Ma'am, do you hear me?" The doctor seemed annoyed, glancing first at her and then toward Herbran.

"Yes." She forced herself to the present. "It's catching."

Scared was how she felt today. Anything but smug. What if Mabel choked to death the way Jeb had two weeks ago? What if there needed to be another funeral? Would it seem like a party to everyone else?

"What can we do?" Herbran wanted to know.

"You have to keep her warm. Give her something to drink—nothing with milk. It makes more phlegm. She'll be better in three or four days or . . ."

"Or what?" Celia asked, a strange staccato quality to her voice.

"Or she'll die. Many die. Some are lucky."

The doctor reached for his coat. Celia had followed him silently to the door. He closed it behind him, leaving a pocket of icy air in the kitchen. She punched down the heap of bread dough that sat on the small table next to the cook stove, mumbling softly to herself.

"What, Mama?" Mabel's voice seemed still weaker today. "Read to me, Mama. Be to me."

She pulled up a chair alongside the crib and sat down, pulling the younger girl in her lap.

"Hurts, Mama. Is Mabel real sick? Does her throat hurted, too?" Alma asked.

"Yes, Baby. I'm pulling these two chairs together and

putting this blanket on them so you can rest here."

And the kitchen, usually cheerful and fragrant, became a sort of infirmary.

The morning droned on, a strange mixture of bottled-up tears and fresh loaves of bread. She prepared food for the men and laid cool cloths on the girls' burning foreheads, moving about on watery legs.

"Shall I stay the afternoon with you? asked Herbran as he finished eating.

She mimicked his practicality.

"No. It won't change anything."

An imaginary clothespin was pinching the space between her eyebrows.

She couldn't decide what was happening. She was mostly frightened. But tired, too. Fatigue ate at her until she felt all swallowed up. Outside it kept snowing.

"You need some rest," said Herbran. Herbran—always knowing what to do. He took her hand and led her into the bedroom and set up two beds for the girls in the corner.

"Now we can be right here with them," he said.

She sank gratefully into her bed.

She awakened, startled. How had she dared to sleep with the child so sick? It was still night. She groped for the side of the bed and crossed the room, a slim, white ghostly image in her muslin gown. Herbran was sitting in the chair by the cribs. He reached for her in the dim lamplight. But she knew already. Mabel's bed was silent.

As she screamed, Alma began to whimper. The room tipped around her, like tea in a saucer, and she fell back into her pillow.

"Where are you going?" she screamed at Herbran later.

It seemed a month later. Actually, it was only a few minutes. He was putting on his clothes.

"To town," he said, flatly.

"Town!" she screeched. "Have you taken leave of your senses? Mabel is dead and you're going to town!"

"Celia, I have to. I have to walk to town to buy a casket. I'll tell the neighbors the news on my way."

"Oh."

That awful word. How ugly it is when children die. Like it's not the right course of events. Disorderly. Backwards, somehow.

Pain gripped her and, like childbirth, hung onto her for an eternity. Then it blessedly released its hold, only to return moments later. Again, like labor pains—only this time, no reward. Nothing to work for. Squeeze and release. Squeeze and release.

Bluntly, she did it all by going through the motions. Like a marionette, she comforted Alma and punched the bread dough.

She pumped the water from the cistern, habitually counting the number of strokes. Fifteen today. She filled a basin and laid her lifeless daughter on the couch and washed her body slowly.

"Mama, what are you doing?"

Alma's curiosity seemed to push forward through her pallor.

"I'm washing Mabel. Then I have to fix her hair so she looks real nice for when the people come."

She reached for the white organdy dress that she had hung on the curtain rod and slipped it over Mabel's head.

"Is it a party, Mama?"

A hint of excitement punctured Alma's voice.

"No, darling. It's a funeral. Maybe sometimes it's sort of like a party," she added, bitterly.

"I feel so sick, Mama."

Celia rushed to her younger daughter. Yes, she was definitely weaker. Panicking, she picked her up and held her close. Her body felt floppy and hot—a direct contrast to the cold, still one on the couch.

"Mama," whispered Alma, her voice barely audible.
"Yes?"
Celia held her breath.
"I want to wear my white dress, too," said Alma in all her four-year-old wisdom, "when you wash me and I go to the party."

She saw him, at last, round the corner by the road. How she used to love the graceful curve of the oaks on that corner. What did it matter now? What did anything matter? How could she tell him? He walked slowly, tiredly. The small pine box balanced on his square shoulders.

Stiffly, she greeted him at the door.
"You have to go back," she said.
"Back? I don't understand."
"We need another one," she said, woodenly.

The wind whipped up her legs, throwing the door open behind her, and he saw what he needed to see. Wordlessly, he turned and she watched him walk away, listening to his feet crunching in the snow.

As a young mother and a clinic nurse, I realized I was overreacting when parents refused immunization injections for their children. Then I remembered the story my father had told me about his sisters who had died from diphtheria. This is my grandmother's story.

Marie Erickson Saterbak

MY SURPRISING SISTER

From the moment I saw her drinking the corn colored milk from our mother's full bosom, my sister Marie changed my life.

For I was "the oldest and the youngest," my father said.

Early, Marie and I developed a mutual trust. At nine months, she sat confidently in my bicycle basket when we went for a ride to visit the neighbors. She smiled while holding my left hand, my right hand on the handlebars. We were nearly at their driveway when the wheel skidded in the gravel. I felt that same skidding in my chest. Her small hand still trusting mine, I walked the bike up the driveway and after a short visit, all the way home. I was one scared twelve-year-old.

I felt proud when she modeled the red and white checked gingham dress I made in home ec. It had puffed sleeves and puffed pockets. When the curly-haired three-year-old passed the reviewing stand, everyone applauded.

Ten years later, Marie modeled her own creation at the county 4-H style show. Chosen Junior Style Queen, she was the envy of all the boys when she was kissed by Miss America, Minnesota's Beebe Shoppe. Marie cartwheeled from the house to the barn, preferring to play with the kittens and puppies rather than dolls. Most pictures from her childhood are taken with dogs, kittens or chickens.

Marie oriented Mother when she returned to the one-room country school during the teaching shortage of the forties. Mother said she never would have made the transition back to teaching without her help.

Tears of happiness stung my cheeks when Marie, graduating as salutatorian, delivered a well-organized speech at her high school commencement.

Two college boys roomed at our house and I invited Marie and her girlfriend, with the boys, for dinner. It was a gourmet meal — tuna fish casserole with cheese pinwheel biscuits.

Three years later, she graduated from nursing school and a few weeks later married Lowell, one of those young men.

After more than twenty years of nursing, Marie returned to school, earning a degree in Interior Design. Soon after graduation, she opened her business, Prism Interiors, and has demonstrated both her creativity and business acumen.

My sister, a born motivator, has inspired not only her son, Paul, and daughter, Andrea, to make their dreams a reality but has encouraged me to start writing.

Recently I found the birthday book Dad gave me when I was ten years old. This is the entry on September 28 of the following year:

"My darling sister Marie CeCelia is born. It is the happiest and most important day of my life."

LIVING A NIGHTMARE

I dial 911 and hear a non-human voice. A robot voice. Nonexpressive and uncompassionate. The voice recites the menu: If you have a touch tone phone, press one. If this is a life and death emergency, press two. If this is a domestic argument, press three. If there is a burglar, press four. If you suspect a rapist, press five.

Choking on a piece of steak, I am trying to call 911 at the same time as attempting a Heimlich maneuver by pressing my epigastric area on the kitchen counter.

I stay on the line until I hear a dispassionate voice, "If you'd like to make a call, hang up and dial your operator."

Again, I dial 911 and pound my coffee cup on the counter in an attempt to communicate. The operator hangs up.

Feeling faint and dizzy, I somehow make it to the door. Luckily, a neighbor, passing by, sees what she later called my "blue moon face."

She runs to dial 911. In less than two minutes the paramedics are giving me an effective Heimlich maneuver.

Since then, I have begun a crusade to rehumanize America by banning all prerecorded voices. No more robots. I am agitating for humans who live, breathe, love and hate as I do—with real voices.

By letter, fax machine and telephone, I contact large corporations and Congressmen, small companies as well as anyone who will listen.

With determination, I will make this change in America.

I yearn to return to the "good old days," when an operator called "Central" or more informally, Emma, worked in front of a small town switchboard. She spoke in a pleasant voice as she said, "Number, please," after which she connected my call. If I had questions, she answered them with honesty and humor. She even blew the noon whistle and the 10 P.M. curfew.

Perhaps there is hope for change. I smile when I read that the latest mind boggling robot is named Emma. She also may blow a 10 p.m. curfew.

It is difficult for me to believe this is all a nightmare.

A RED BOX OF MEMORIES

The weathered red box has interest and intrigue. It holds secrets and souvenirs from a long life. My life. Its black velvet lining is worn smooth with the years.

I smile to see Mother's watch, a prenuptial gift, its stem broken, its crystal cracked but its white gold case as new.

I open a letter from a homesick student. Me. It is as if it is written from another self. A few snapshots of high school friends are scattered throughout the box. A treasured bookmark is tucked into a white, nurses' New Testament, a gift at graduation from the Gideons. The blue garter from my wedding, its elastic still strong, holds letters of love from my fiancé.

A baptismal scroll, tied with a faded pink ribbon, attests to its age. Next to it is a certificate of graduation from eighth grade. I received it proudly, knowing I was to embark on the adventure of an "adult" life.

My baby shoe, black patent and cracked, lies in the palm of my hand. In its toe, I find an earring set with a diamond. If anyone finds its mate, will they recognize its worth?

I page through a birthday book, a gift from my father containing birthdates of people who were important in my little girl life. I spend time reading the childish writing in an autograph album.

Carefully replacing these treasures, I close the lid and place the box back on the shelf.

For another ten years.

TREADING ON THIN ICE

"Just talk about yourself for five minutes. Introduce yourself. Simple."

These were my instructions when I joined Toastmasters International and was told I had to give an "Ice Breaker" speech.

Talk about myself? What can I say? Do I talk about my successes or my failures? My mouth turns dry as ashes when I think of it. Giving a speech makes even strong people weak in their knees. On a scale of one to ten, I'd rate myself a six—on a good day.

I remembered a painful experience.

"Why don't you say something, Angie? Has the cat got your tongue?"

My mind was empty of any conversational lead.

Possibly because I am a Norwegian-American, it takes me at least five years going on six to let anyone know the "real" me—who thinks and feels. The vulnerable me. It is impossible to break this habit in five minutes.

Where do I begin? At birth or at age 21? Must I tell my birth year? Never. Certainly not to these toastmasters who weren't alive at the time.

Now I understand why it is called an icebreaker speech; it reminds me of the rubber ice when small ponds form from the spring runoff and freeze overnight. Walking on the ice, it bends and cracks. If you don't hurry, you'll be in water up to your knees. Even deeper.

I prepare my speech. I'll tell them my interests and

hobbies and how many children I have. That's safe. Shall I tell them I am a risk taker? This is not necessary because I've demonstrated my risk taking by joining a Toaster Masters Club at my age. (That unmentionable age).

I'll tell how Mother said I was born during a windy duststorm and have been running ever since. That sounds cute. True, too.

Should I mention what I was doing during the historical happenings like Pearl Harbor or when J.F.K. was shot? That should be good for at least one minute.

I smile and begin writing my speech.

"I was born an Erickson from Rollag, Minnesota. One of five Erickson girl cousins—all except one had first names which started with the letter 'A' ."

I dress carefully in a conservative blue suit with a white tailored blouse and gold lapel pin. I just might look like a Republican were it not the lapel pin is a donkey with emerald eyes.

I think of a student in my college speech class who shook so violently that I held my knees in sympathy. I wonder how he would react to an icebreaker speech. He probably wouldn't live through it but the question is, will I?

I notice all nineteen toastmasters seated at the table look expectant. They look as if they want me to succeed. I think, *Someday these folks will be my friends.*

Introduced by the toastmaster of the evening, I walk to the podium, supported by spongy legs and adjust the mike. My tongue sticks to the roof of my mouth. However, I smile and concentrate on three friendly faces. I remember hearing President Eisenhower imagined his audience in their underwear—then they no longer terrified him.

My shaking knees, hidden behind the lectern, my voice firm, I begin, "Madam Toastmaster, Honored Guests, Fellow Toastmasters."

NO

"No," is a difficult word.
Short, no nonsense,
a word I dislike,
but a word I sometimes use,
a word I understand,
although it sounds autocratic,
dogmatic and crude.

"No" is a necessary word.
It protects
and brings space.
It sets limits
and defines ideals.
It defends and unites
the whole human race.

ANOTHER BIRTHDAY PEEK

Next birthday I'll be peeking on tiptoe
into old age.
I compare my landmark thirty-ninth
when I peeked into middle age.
Peeking into the next decade
is a birthday habit,
for each decade holds its magic,
a mystery to unfold.
Life's challenges are still here
and the same things delight me.
Someday I'll peek into my final decade
to the magic of another world.

OF LILACS AND PUNISHMENT

Mother complained that the lilacs obscured her view from the kitchen window; therefore, Dad and his hired man, with ax, crowbar and energy, grubbed the bushes leaving but a small clump near the kitchen door.

This small clump doubled in size within a few years. Covered with pale purple fragrant flowers, it became the "bloomingest" bush in our neighborhood.

Dad loved lilacs and brought armsful into the house. Lilacs filled the fruit jar vases in the kitchen, living room, front porch and bedrooms; only the pantry survived without a bouquet.

My father subscribed to the "spare the rod, spoil the child," theory of discipline. He hung a bare lilac branch behind the kitchen door. A branch used only for punishment. My punishment. If I were disobedient or spunky, he looked meaningfully at the kitchen corner. He rarely used the branch. However, I grew to dislike the sight and smell of lilacs.

Plants, as humans, have a sixth sense because the lilac bush at our lake cottage is dwarfed and never blooms. It is aware that I dislike it. Perhaps it needs pruning, a branch removed to hang behind the kitchen door—as a reminder to grandchildren.

WEATHERING THE WEATHER

"*You don't need a weatherman to know which way the wind blows.*"
"Subterranean Homesick Blues" (1965)

Everyone's hero, the weatherman, is a "king of the castle," who is "bigger than life." Both clichés apt, as many young, old and middle-aged watch the 10 p.m. newscast solely for the weather report.

Men and women weather forecasters are as familiar as family. They speak at art exhibits and banquets, all in the hope of taming the weather.

This is a false hope because clouds perpetually roam the sky. Most folks worry about a catastrophe when they see angrily swirling clouds over their rooftops.

You are one such catastrophier; however, you are confused over which is eminent—a tornado watch or warning. You obsess about this terminology until you see an ominous black cloud with a descending nipple floating in the afternoon sky. You stop obsessing and run for cover.

During summer in the Southwest, the temperature may rise to 120 degrees. When the plastic steering wheel in your car melts in your hand, it's proof you can fry French toast on the sidewalk. The humidity is so low your skin feels as tissue paper or, even worse, burlap.

The community pools teem with swimmers of all ages and sizes. Later, they gather near the television to hear of record-breaking heat.

Winter, in its vagaries, consumes you; at least four months you are preoccupied with reading the thermometer.

"Twenty-two below today."

Preoccupied? You bet. When ice crystals form on your eyelids and your feet freeze in sheepskin-lined boots, it's cold.

Your favorite wintertime reading is the *Farmer's Almanac*. It is comforting to read of previous extremes of temperature and realize that the earth still turns on its axis.

You worry about the money wasted on long distance phone calls when you discuss in minute detail every twist and turn of the weather. This may include a recent rain, an approaching snowstorm, a blocked Interstate or a swollen river lapping at your back step. These long distance calls start out with, "How's the weather?" Then as an afterthought, "How are you doing?"

As blizzards blow, you look out a window and see the snow as in the round glass globe which, when you shake it, obscures the scene.

During these blizzards, schools are cancelled and youngsters build elaborate snowforts and snowmen. They roll and slide down snowdrifts.

Besides the children, the ski hill operators rejoice as there is no need to manufacture the white stuff.

The winter of '97 proved to be fodder for talk shows well into the summer. Record snowfall and low temperatures followed by flooding created new heroes and burnished everyone's survival skills.

After the cleanup, neighbors gather for coffee and visit about—the weather. Card parties proliferate but participants pause long enough to listen to the 10 p.m. weather forecast.

"For it is always fair weather when good fellows get together."

Richard Hovey (1898)

DO PICTURES LIE?

As I look at a picture of myself, I rationalize that pictures amplify size and distort features. Yet, I am upset for one long and dismal day.

Worse yet, when I go to my husband for comfort, he says the wrong things.

"You look great—natural," he smiles reassuringly.

I tell him to keep quiet only I say it in the vernacular.

I've heard pictures don't lie and I believe it because my husband, children and grandchildren all look handsome on a picture taken around the Thanksgiving dinner table.

It's hard to tell me from the turkey.

WHATEVER HAPPENED TO APRONS?

Once upon a time, mothers and daughters wore apron-covered dresses. The large aprons, which protected housedresses, were called "Mother Hubbards." Whereas, ruffled half aprons, usually made from organdy, were tied at the waist of their "Sunday" dresses.

Mother wore look-alike aprons every day of the week—except Sunday. These aprons, as backless dresses, covered her dress from neckline to hemline in front, its straps criss-crossing across the back.

All her aprons were made from flour sack material. She purchased flour in fifty-pound sacks which came in a variety of colors and prints. This flour-covered fabric required washing and rewashing.

Following the final rinse, she pinned the cloth to a rope clothes line tied between two oak trees. It appeared as a colorful kite floating in the prairie breeze. After it was dry, she sprinkled it with water and rolled it in a towel for a few hours before ironing it.

Pinning a pattern made from brown butcher paper on the cloth, she carefully cut around the paper. Then she covered the raw edges with bias tape. Mother preferred a contrasting color tape because she said matching the tape and the fabric made a dull and uninteresting apron.

She fashioned large, strong pockets, big enough to transfer misplaced objects from one room to another. These pockets always bulged.

Each week Mother donned a clean housedress, handmade from these same flour sacks. They sported a sweetheart neckline and buttoned past the waist. No zippers. She covered this with a giant apron, clean for the day, and when unexpected company drove in the long driveway, she quickly changed to a fresh apron.

I, too, wore aprons. Mine always had a ruffle on the shoulder and a chicken or rabbit embroidered on the pocket.

My favorite apron was given to me at my cousin's wedding when I waited on tables. It was trimmed with lace and tied in a huge bow at the waist.

Rarely do I see aprons anymore. They look strange worn over shorts or slacks.

But when I am alone in the kitchen, I knot a dishtowel around my waist.

It looks great.

LAUGHTER

Give the gift of laughter to one person every day and in a year you will have brought joy to 365 people. If you laugh with them, 730 people will be joyful.

Laughter is contagious. It is more contagious than the common cold. It is passed without a cough or a sneeze. It may be passed in spite of a cough or sneeze.

From the gurgling laugh of a baby to Grandpa's chuckle, a laugh is heartwarming. It spans generations and aids communication.

Laughter at oneself is therapeutic whereas laughter at others is cruel.

To laugh as one works hastens the task and shortens the day. It boosts production and prevents accidents.

Laughter is fun, grand hilarious fun. It has even been known to make friends out of strangers.

ONE OF A PAIR

Marriages and shoes have much in common. Both are a pair. But whoever heard of a pair of shoes which don't match? A mismatched pair would be discarded quicker than they could walk to the altar.

Shoes, as marriages, are diverse. Frivolous party shoes are made for show and beauty but the wearer may find them uncomfortable—unable to walk. This, in contrast to sturdy walking shoes which, as comfortable spouses, married more than twenty years, grow old together.

Classic pumps may be compared to conventional marriages where children and pets thrive.

Sandals are like marriages which allow space and freedom of expression. Each individual may develop special interests and be on their own! However, they walk in sync, treasuring their diversity.

New shoes, as new marriages, tend to pinch. The feet need a massage at the close of the day. Time takes care of the problem and soon the shoe conforms to the foot and the couple complement each other.

Occasionally, a pair of shoes is impossible to wear. This is noticeable from the beginning. They are discarded for the welfare of the foot. Misfit marriages may end in divorce, hopefully, salvaging both individuals.

Heel height may demonstrate power and success. Low heels, moderate success. Higher heels rise to pinnacles of power which can be easily toppled.

Shoe polish keeps the leather supple and shining, even as generosity and forbearance make a gleaming marriage, a marriage which may become as comfortable as an old shoe.

IN PRAISE OF TV

Bad mouthing television is a popular national pastime for intellectuals and wanna-be intellectuals. Although thousands blame the ills of the world on the "tube," many are hypocritical and watch it six to eight hours a day.

My parents watched "Groucho Marx" and the "Brady Bunch" from a small circular screen implanted into a large walnut cabinet. These early shows were televised live—warts and all.

Today's news is tomorrow's history as documented by the news coverage of the war in Viet Nam, the first televised war, showing spectacles of horror.

I watched the Eisenhower inauguration on my black and white screen. Later, I was shocked and grieved to watch President Kennedy's funeral procession.

True, at times TV is out of control. Raunchy situation comedies and salacious talk shows appear to take over the networks.

But there is a television menu for all—from evangelistic crusades to cable news—from public television to naughty movies. And more. It is our choice.

We watch investigative news programs until we are afraid to eat chicken or take a car in for repair.

Advertisements take us into the kitchens and bathrooms of America. Some of these ads amuse while others repel us. But when we shop, we remember the product we have seen advertised. Seeing, hearing and reading about a product really does spur us to purchase it.

It is impossible to imagine life without a TV set. I listen to wondrous programs over television in our rural area, far from the metropolitan cities of New York and Washington. Life without television would be worse than a life without indoor plumbing.

Yes, I like TV.

YOUR FIRST GRAY HAIR

Is it lint, angel hair from the Christmas tree or a sunbeam gone awry? You examine this hair from all angles and finally, with a thumping and thudding heart, you pluck it from your head. The truth is inescapable. It is a gray hair.

You sit down and re-examine this gray hair. It appears like a wiry white thread among the dark hairs on your head. It is such a strong hair, you realize it will soon be part of an army of gray determined to invade and conquer your entire head.

You are stunned when you recognize you are old—all of thirty-eight. Then your mind goes on fast forward. You see yourself as a grandparent, your head topped with silver.

You remember your grandmother wearing her hair in a "pug" on top of her head. It has been years since you've seen anyone wear this hairstyle, certainly not anyone your age.

You hunt for a second gray hair; mercifully, you don't find any but all day your mind returns to that one gray hair. You wish it had come out in your hairbrush, hidden among the dark hairs.

Finally, at the close of the day, you relax and rationalize, "What's one gray hair?"

ANOTHER FOUR-LETTER WORD

Home is a four-letter word. A word full of wonder and wisdom. A word overflowing with memories, happiness—even heartache.

You barely remember your first home. The home where you took your first steps, wobbly steps between your parents' outstretched arms. You wish you could remember those steps as you imagine the proud, beaming smiles of your parents.

You remember more clearly the home of your childhood, a humble home during the Great Depression. The kitchen was covered with a linoleum rug and the living room covered with an Axminster carpet, a dusty rug as the carpet sweeper didn't extract all the dust of the Thirties and there was no money for a vacuum cleaner.

You remember the round oak table with claw feet which expanded to seat more than a dozen people at Thanksgiving and Christmas.

Dorm rooms and apartments followed. The apartments were cold in the winter and warm in the summer and sometimes the other way around.

Your first house became a home for you, your husband and your children. It was full of laughter and occasional tears.

Then your child's first steps came on the living room floor which later doubled as a gymnasium.

Homes change just as you change over the years.

POTATO DAYS

It is Labor Day, 1953 in potato growing country and Barnesville, Minnesota celebrates.

This is a gala celebration with a potato picking contest, a parade, free potato soup and a dance in the evening at the fairgrounds.

My husband and his friend enter the potato picking contest. Nine pair of pickers form a line at the end of a field of potatoes. The freshly dug spuds lay glistening in rows in the black soil.

A shotgun start. Thirty-six hands grasp the potatoes and place them in wire baskets. When the baskets are full, they empty them into burlap sacks. Within a few minutes, there is an army of potato sacks standing tall in the field.

My husband and his partner work fast and hard but don't place in the contest. They are good losers, delighted to be in the upper third of the pickers and vow to enter and win the contest next year.

His new gold gloves are dirty and there are holes in the palms of the right glove. I notice the dirt has sifted through the fabric to his hands.

My mother-in-law, my sister, three sons, my husband and I visit my husband's aunt this Labor Day. We, with hundreds of others, eat the cream of potato soup, topped with onion—after which we line Main Street to watch the parade.

Our five-year-old son becomes lost in the crowd. I

entertain guilty thoughts of poor mothering. I should have kept him at my side with the baby and the toddler. I know it is all my fault because my husband is tired from the picking so I can't expect him to watch the child.

Suddenly, the loud speaker blares, "Lost boy at the grandstand. He says his name is Mike."

Embarrassed but relieved, we find him eating a strawberry ice cream cone. It is his first encounter with a policeman.

Weary, we return to rest at Auntie's house. Two sons fall asleep on the sofa. Baby Douglas is sleeping in a basket which rests between two dining room chairs and my sister is curled into a small ball in the easy chair. I wonder if she is asleep or merely marking time.

Suddenly, the two oldest boys awaken and begin to race around the living room. They overturn the basket with the sleeping baby. I pick him up and cradle him, thankful for his steady breathing.

We eat a late dinner in the dining room. A low wattage bulb hangs from a black braided card and barely lights the faded rose flowered walls.

Auntie Flo is coming home with us and we wait for her to pack. It is an hour after midnight before the crowded station wagon pulls out of the driveway.

My stomach, still full of potato soup, churns as I recall the long day's events.

COMPLIMENTS

Please don't give me a compliment.
I can't stand praise.
It sends me into tailspins of fear.
It chokes my self-esteem.
Don't tell me I'm an angel,
like my name.
The darkest side of my
    nature rears its head—
threatening to reveal all my secrets.
For I am of Nordic descent,
guaranteed to turn off praise.

A PURSE FOR EVERY OUTFIT

Once upon a time, and perhaps some women still honor this tradition, a woman had a purse for every outfit. The shoes and purse were dyed to match.

Purses ranged in color from burgundy and green to brown, gray and black. Still do.

I like black purses. My perennial favorite is a large, black leather purse which opens as a satchel. It is large enough to hold three books and a legal pad in addition to my makeup and billfold. Ideal for travel. It holds anything you can't get on a plane any other way.

My friend carries everything one ever wanted or needed in her purse. It is a miniature five and dime store. A supermarket purse which has magnificent fold-out pockets, zipper side pockets and a pull-out snap purse on the end of a string. I have never seen anything like it.

When I shop with my friend, if a stocking runs, she has nail polish; a headache, she has aspirin; a safety pin for a rip— and so on. I am both impressed and intimidated because my usual small, black, utilitarian clutch contains a comb, lipstick, tissue, compact and billfold.

Mother had an all-season purse. Always black. When it became shabby, she replaced it with another like it. Her purses had a division down the middle with a zippered closing. This contained a few dollars and small change. For Dad carried their money.

Last summer I bought a lovely straw purse at my

favorite store. One wearing and it fell apart. I returned it for another just like it. The second one had the same defect as the first. The store owner phoned the the company and in a short time I received the most beautiful summer purse I have ever owned. For free. My friend, the store owner, felt I had suffered enough with the purses and the wholesaler had listened.

In my very long life, I notice things really do go in cycles so I expect sometime in the new millennium we will become more formal in our attire and wear matching shoes, hats, gloves and purses.

When I'm out with my husband, I rarely take my purse. I am unencumbered. My lipstick, compact and comb lie flat in his suit pocket. For he, as my father, carries the money.

DRESSED FOR THE OCCASION

I remember life affirming and life shattering events by the dress I wore that day.

When I was five I wore a burgundy satin handmade dress with an eggshell Peter Pan collar and lacy gold buttons. Mother made it over from a dress from her teaching days. The photographer captured me in that dress as I stood by a little black chair. That picture is proudly hanging at our lake cottage.

At Confirmation I wore an angel white dress. It was a crisp October day and before the next summer I had outgrown it. But I'm nurse comfortable in white, my uniform for forty years.

My son was killed in a car accident. I wore a navy dress with white trim.

Another navy blue dress was worn at my only piano recital. I forgot much of my music that day and I have forgotten what happened to that dress.

I rarely wear navy. It is not a happy color for me.

I had a lovely red silk dress with a ruffled neckline and cuffs which I gave later to my mom. She wore it the last Christmas we spent together. At 91, she sang Christmas carols with a strong voice and great enthusiasm. The next summer Mother's funeral was a celebration of her life. The recessional was the *Hallelujah Chorus*. Appropriately, Mother wore that red dress.

Green is my favorite color. I wore green on my first date. One of my favorite dresses is a sage green coat dress. More than ten years old, it is still a favorite dress.

The first day of high school my aunt took a picture of me in a red and white checked dress Mother had fashioned with puff sleeves and a sweetheart neckline. It was trimmed with red rickrack.

I, the Maid of Honor at my sister's wedding, wore a white crinoline dress with a bronze sash and carried matching bronze mums with a cascading sheaf of wheat. It was a beautiful wedding - I felt beautiful too as I had lost twenty pounds for the occasion.

I have a dress in my closet I have never worn and look forward with expectation to the memory of wearing that dress to a special event.

EARLY BIRDS

Pale lavender hangs over the rippled
waters of the lake.
The mist is low on the hillside.
Chattering, contented birds gather
the early worms of the day
as I stretch to see the dawn.

BETWEEN SIPS

These days I'm drinking water. Lots of water. It goes a long way toward filling my stomach and staving off hunger pangs. It goes a long way but not always long enough. I still get hungry.

For as long as I can remember, and every year I remember a longer time, I have been on a diet.

Sometimes that diet has been successful—I have pictures to prove it. I have even framed a couple of those pictures.

I can still hear Mother's muffled voice, her mouth full of pins as she fitted a skirt on me, "Those hips!"

However, throughout the years, I have come to terms with "those hips," along with a few other aberrations.

Each time I attempt a new diet, I become enamored with the latest cookbook displayed at a bookstore. Especially those books where the food is photographed in glorious color. Therefore I have a cookbook collection and a pound of fat gained from each book in that collection.

I also collect exercise records and books. At times I paste a favorite exercise on my bathroom mirror. Only one problem. I wait until the next day to start exercising.

If a diet is successful after the first ten pound loss, my family and friends take notice of the new me emerging from the tent of fat.

"Are you sick?" a friend inquires.

"You look tired," another pronounces.

Yes, I am both sick and tired of being fat and it is time to put more ice and lemon in my water. After all, it does satiate my hunger.

TABLECLOTHS

Recently I bought a marvelous cross-stitched linen tablecloth at my favorite antique shop. It is large enough to seat eight at my dining room table and for proof it has eight matching napkins. A treasure.

It reminds me of earlier treasures. Mother embroidered lunch cloths she placed kitty-corner on the table between meals. In order to write, I had to turn back a corner. One day I tipped my inkwell onto a snowy square of embroidered linen. Mother graciously soothed my guilts and soaked the ink spot in milk until it disappeared. After this episode, I became a more careful writer.

My favorite tablecloth is lace, crocheted by my mother. It is elegant and I use it on special occasions with the best china and silver. It transforms plain food into gourmet, fit for royalty.

A round table in the sundrenched corner of our Arizona room is covered with a white and black polka dot cloth which skims the floor. Twelve beautiful pictures of our grandchildren are grouped on it. This makes the table unique.

However, the most memorable lunch cloth is a poorly sewn blue and white checked cloth with hemstitched fringes and four matching napkins which I made in an art class in elementary school.

When I finished the cloth I realized I would never become an artist and decided I would plan a career in nursing.

That little blue tablecloth changed my life.

SWEET SCENTS

I delight entering my favorite department store near the perfume counter. The scents are sweet. The displays intriguing. I can't resist trying a variety of perfumes. One spray to each arm, one to each ear and a quick spritz into the air.

Walking through this haze of perfume, I remember sixty years earlier receiving a gift of perfume from Aunt Dora.

Three small barrel shaped bottles of lilac, jasmine and sweet pea perfume were tucked into a green baseball-sized dome topped holder, supported by three spindly feet.

It was my favorite Christmas gift.

I am always delighted with a gift of perfume. Each year Bill gives me perfume in my Christmas stocking and I have stockpiled a grand variety.

For I use perfume sparingly. Only on special occasions.

Recently I took inventory of my perfume bottles. Big bottles and little bottles. Purple bottles and calico printed bottles. A red triangular bottle and a crystal decanter. All feminine, all beautiful. I placed them on a mirror in the bathroom where I can look at them.

Perhaps I'll start using perfume daily, thus making each day a special occasion.

Won't Bill be pleased?

LOST AND FOUND

Eight-year-old Pat had a grocery sack half-filled with leaves when he caught his boat under an exposed root and crashed to the ground. The pain was excruciating. His left ankle puffed up quickly and he started to cry. He knew he was unable to walk.

Pat and his faithful black Lab, Smoky, had been walking several hours. The Jamieson family lived five miles from the woods. Pat had parked his bike on the road leading into the woods because he was collecting leaves for his science leaf collection.

"Smoky, Smoky, get help."

He patted the dog's head and after a few minutes Smoky disappeared, following a faint trail through the woods.

Pat, an excellent student, carried a four-point average. His two brothers were athletic but Pat was a little clumsy. It wasn't the first time he had taken a bad fall.

He huddled under a tree trying to get into a position to ease the pain in his ankle. He removed his shoe because it was getting too tight.

Pat thought of many things, mostly food and his comfortable room overlooking the creek. He wondered if this is how it felt to die. A lonesome, lonesome time. He prayed.

The sun set and it was becoming dark. Very dark. Dampness penetrated his clothes. He wondered how soon he would die.

Finally, he fell asleep.

It was sunrise and Sara Conroy stretched and got out of bed. She thought she heard noise outside the house. Her husband Paul was still sleeping.

Sara threw on a warm red flannel robe because the log cabin was cold on fall mornings. She entered the kitchen and heard a bark, accompanied by urgent scratching at the door.

A black Lab stood on the step.

Sara, a veterinary science major, loved animals and patted the dog, coaxing him into the kitchen. She poured a bowl of water which he drank eagerly but continued to whimper and scratch at the floor with his paws.

"Paul, wake up, someone must be lost in the woods."

"Ah, what did you say?" Paul groggily answered.

"There's a black lab in the kitchen, very upset, like he's trying to tell me something."

"Oh, Sara — dogs don't talk."

"Hurry, Paul," her voice became stern.

Hearing the change in his wife's usual calm manner, Paul dressed quickly.

Smoky tugged at her pocket as if to say, "Hurry up before it's too late."

The dog led Paul and Sara out of the clearing and into the woods. They walked more than a mile until they found a faint trail leading through the bushes. Following Smoky another fifty feet, they found the boy — still huddled under the tree.

Pat couldn't believe it. Smoky had brought help. He tried to sound brave. But all he could do was squawk through parched lips and swollen tongue, "Smoky found you. I'm so cold and my foot feels numb."

"Honey, we're here to help you."

Sara put her arm around the shaking child to comfort him.

"Sara, you support his ankle while I hoist him on my

back and shoulder in a fireman's hold."

"What's your name?" she asked.

"Pat, Pat Jamieson. Don't forget my leaf collection in the brown bag."

Pat thought he must be dreaming or perhaps he had died and gone to heaven when he saw the Hansel and Gretel log cabin in the clearing. It was the first log cabin he had ever seen—outside of pictures.

"A log cabin. Cool."

"Yes," Paul said, "Sara and I have always wanted to live in one."

"So we are building it," Sara added.

Paul smiled, "It's lots of work but we love it."

"We are trying to finish it before we have a family, a boy, someone like you," and Sara brushed the tangled red hair from the boy's brow.

"Rest on the couch while I fix you some food. You must be starved."

He was drowsing when he heard a knock on the door.

"Officer Janice Kirby. Have you seen an eight-year-old boy? His parents reported him missing last night and I found his bike at the edge of the woods."

Pat ate a peanut butter and jelly sandwich while the officer phoned the Jamiesons to tell them of their son's rescue.

"His ankle needs treatment. I'll bring him to the doctor at Timberlane. You can meet us there. Yes, he seems fine, other than his ankle."

Pat hugged and thanked the Conroys before he left. He knew he would never forget their kindness.

Smoky beside him, Pat sat with his ankle propped on a pillow in the back seat of the police car.

He had always thought police were big strong men—but this was a pretty lady. Almost as pretty as his mother. Thinking of his mother made him cry.

Yes, policemen did much more than arrest murderers and bank robbers; they also rescued lost children, he thought.

The ankle was only a bad sprain and the doctor secured it with an elastic ace bandage. Pat thanked Officer Kirby for her help before she drove away in her car.

After hugs and kisses with his family, Pat said, "Mom—Dad—I'm going to be a policeman when I grow up and I'm going to live in a log cabin."

TWO DEAR DEER

We two mothers sat disconsolate in the living room. Both of us had lost our sons two weeks apart and a mutual friend had brought us together to comfort one another.

Our sons both died under car wheels. A sudden death—no chance to say, "I love you," or even "Goodbye."

The coffee on the table grew cold, the cookies untouched, as we sat there wrapped in our misery.

I looked up to see two fawn standing head to head, a foot away from the window.

They were beautiful fawn. Seeing them brought me peace. Never before had I seen two deer looking in a window.

It was as if our sons were consoling us.

CHEERS FOR COFFEE

The coffee brewing in your kitchen is the coziest and most tranquilizing sound in your world.

Coffee is the most cozy at dawn when the great blue heron browses the waterfront and you hear a chorus of smaller birds near your kitchen window.

The anticipation of a cup of coffee converts an otherwise dreary day into paradise. Coffee is the most tranquilizing when your brain is stressed at the close of the day. It makes troubles evaporate and psychic pain less powerful.

It is hard to separate the taste from the smell of coffee. Indescribable.

Drinking coffee is a delight. An adventure. At home it is predictable. Hot and strong. It runs the gamut in a restaurant from lukewarm colored water to as thick and opaque as mud.

At times you serve it in thin porcelain cups at a ladies' luncheon. Other times you serve it in heavy lipped mugs with a logo on its side. Some of your friends dilute it with skim milk, others with cream. Still others sweeten it with sugar or substitute.

Coffee assumes a different persona poured from a thermos in your car. You rationalize it will keep you awake and alert while driving.

Coffee and conversation just evolve. Truly, most secrets are revealed over a cup of coffee.

Some buy coffee beans and grind their own. Many of

these beans have a gourmet taste. You consider yourself a coffee purist. A connoisseur of fine coffee.

In both likely and unlikely places, you find coffee gourmet specialty shops. In grim hospital corridors coffee comforts many awaiting news of a loved one. Placing your hands around a mug of this coffee warms your hands and heart on a dismal day.

In your memory bank is stored Mother's egg coffee, cooked on the kitchen wood range in an aluminum coffee pot with a burnt wooden handle. She tells you it is a wedding gift from over twenty years before.

Coffee boiled over a campfire has a memory all its own. You remember it boiling high and dripping into the flames. You remember singeing the hair on your arms when retrieving it. Gritty with the grounds, it tasted terrific.

You remember the first coffee you drank—heavy with cream and sugar, the way your father liked it. Later, you learn to like it black. Less strong but with a silky, golden appearance.

The abundance of coffee houses proves coffee drinking in its various forms is a national pastime.

Every so many years, there is a caffeine scare. Tests are taken and stories are told of cancer and caffeine. Coffee addiction is worse than cocaine or cigarettes but the scares blow over.

Coffee time is the most memorable time of each day; from dawn to dusk you enjoy its flavor. Cheers for coffee! That most seductive brew!

THE AX MURDER

Saturday morning, Mother, dressed in Dad's red plaid-lined denim jacket went to the chicken house to select a chicken for our Sunday dinner.

This handsome rooster just that day had crowed at dawn, the noise reverberating throughout the house. Little did he know it was to be his swan song on his last day on earth.

I watched, mesmerized, as Mother grasped him by his legs and carried him to a stump in front of the granary. Then my gentle mother picked up the double bit ax and in one well-defined swoop, brought it down on the neck of the chicken.

Its head was severed and its long neck was bent and bleeding over the white feathers on his body.

Mother carried a large aluminum teakettle of boiling water and a pail over to the still warm bird. She poured the water over the feathers and let it stand twenty minutes to half an hour.

The air smelled of wet chicken feathers. Unpleasant.

Then my gentle mother pulled the feathers off the chicken. Her hands flew as did the feathers in the early morning breeze.

I learned more about the anatomy of a chicken from what happened next.

Mother placed the chicken on the chopping board and made a happy face cut under the breast bone with a sharp knife. Then, gently but firmly, she scooped out the insides of that rooster and wrapped them in newspaper.

Quickly, she moved the chicken's body over the flames in the kitchen range. Singeing the pinfeathers, she called it, this smell of burnt flesh even more unpleasant than that of the wet feathers.

I helped her rinse the chicken with many changes of cold water.

Sunday morning, Mother sectioned the chicken neatly with her sharp knife. Legs, thighs, breast, backbone and wings were rolled in flour, salt and pepper; then fried until brown and crisp in half butter, half lard in the large black cast iron skillet.

Never have I tasted so delicious an entree as Mother's fried chicken.

WHY WORRY?

I have an inherited genetic trait. Worry. Mother worried. Grandma worried. I'm told Grandma's mother worried. Therefore, I have learned to lean back, relax and enjoy worrying.

My worries are of various sizes, shapes and contortions, some real, some surreal. They are animate and inanimate. The animate worries are well-defined—persons. The inanimate can be anything my heart desires to worry about.

I've always worried about grades—from first grade to graduate school. With the exception of high school. Somehow, other worries took precedence and I couldn't care or didn't care to worry about grades. My grades reflected this attitude.

In high school, I worried constantly about my appearance. Were my nose and ears abnormally large? Certainly I was heavy but didn't know how to diet. I ate dozens of "Dagwood" sandwiches. A Dagwood sandwich was made of one slice of white bread and one slice of whole wheat (I bought a half and half loaf), lettuce, mayonnaise, pickles, tomatoes and cold cuts. I did "light housekeeping" in one room. Dagwood and I entertained girlfriends frequently.

By the time I was in nursing school, I forgot about the nose and ear worries. World War II was in full force and student nurses, with a handful of R.N. supervisors, ran the hospital. Most nurses were in the Army and Navy.

But I worried about my grades. Somehow, I passed but I'm not sure with "flying colors."

Of course, I worried I would never have a date because most fellows were in the service. I wrote some of my friends and worried they may not get the letters overseas or if they didn't answer quickly, I feared them captured by the Germans or worse yet, dead.

When the war ended, it was far too exciting a time to worry.

Soon after, I started dating the man I would later marry. After the first date, I worried he wouldn't call again. He did. We married a year after that first date.

During the years which followed, I was too busy with four boys and a part-time nursing position to spend time worrying. Of course, I made a few neurotic attempts to worry and sometimes succeeded.

The next twenty years there were real things to worry about. I discovered when things were real, I didn't worry because I was too busy trying to solve the problem.

Now in the starlight years of my life, I worry least of all. It's strange because earlier I would have thought I would worry about the inevitability of death or debilitating disease. Not so.

Most days, I enjoy the process of being alive and the ability to move one foot in front of the other. I have come to terms with the things which cannot be changed and am learning to enjoy dawn, birds and breezes.

Some day, I may even get started with something new to worry about. After all, I'm an expert worrier. It's in my genes.

TEARS

Tears are a natural phenomenon, necessary to the health of the eye. Without natural tears, the eye needs lubrication from a bottle.

Tears signify sadness and happiness. In the span of a day, one may weep from sorrow and cry with joy.

A mother tells a story of her sick child, "The doctor said she could die any minute. Take her to the hospital at once."

She went on to tell of packing the toddler's clothes, crying as she packed.

"Don't ty, Mama," the toddler said, stretching her tiny hand to wipe her mother's eyes.

The mother cried all the harder. She cried more tears when her daughter became well.

We remember the raw tears during the bombing of the Federal Building at Oklahoma City. We cried, too, sharing their heartbreak.

A baby is born and we cry from joy as we touch petal soft skin and count fingers and toes.

Six years later, we cry when he starts first grade.

We cry as he graduates from high school.

We cry when he gets married.

We cry when our first grandchild is born, and the second . . . the sixth.

We endure early morning weeping when a loved one dies and leaves an empty plate at the table.

Truly, tears are necessary and deserving of our respect.

THEATERS, THEN AND NOW

The world's smallest theater? It could have been—this long and narrow walk-in closet off my parents' bedroom.

In this "smallest" theater, I was stage manager, director, usher, and official curtain puller, in addition to playing both female and male leads. I spent hours at the old oak library table perfecting the script for the one act play on narrow lined tablet paper.

Eagerly, I delivered the handwritten invitations for the opening night performance.

I dressed in a costume garnered from a large trunk in front of the closet window. This trunk became my stage.

During performance I achieved star billing, not only in my eyes, but in the eyes and hearts of the audience. This audience of two, who laughed and clapped. My mom and dad.

Memories of these productions surface when I see old theaters renovated. Majestic old theaters, located in downtown shopping districts in large cities and small towns.

Every theater unique. Some with blue sky and twinkling star ceilings. Others featured curving staircases leading nowhere. The large stages were built for traveling vaudeville shows and later, movies.

These stages were encircled by intricate carving and swathed in curtains of the deep colors of red, blue or purple velvet. Ornate light fixtures swayed from the pressed tin ceilings. Balconies abounded. But the seats were of hard, unyielding wood, curved to fit under the knee.

The theater lobbies were enormous, many decorated with clusters of gargoyles or Doric columns. Candy bars and popcorn were not allowed out of the lobby into the theater.

Handsome young men dressed in red or royal blue tailored uniforms were courteous as they ushered patrons to their seats.

These theaters were appropriate settings for the glamorous screen stars in the golden age of movies. No matter the reel was changed or broke halfway through the movie. No matter the sound system screeched. No matter summer evenings were hot and winter evenings cold under those starlit ceilings.

In contrast, the theaters of today are grouped five, six or more, around a central utilitarian lobby where popcorn and soda are still popular. It is evident soda is permitted into the theater because your shoes adhere to a sticky surface. Later, moving to a nonsticky area, you kick a popcorn box with your foot.

In both the new and old theaters, your idle hand may touch a wad of gum under your seat, some wads still moist, others hardened by time.

Now, no newsreels picturing powerful people, with their abnormal fast walking and jerking gestures. No signs, "Please remove your hat." No Mickey or Minnie Mouse cartoons. No "That's all, folks" with Bugs Bunny dancing on the screen.

The seats of the new theaters are padded. They resemble the rocker in your home. The walls, so dark you can't see the acoustical tile ceiling.

In both the new and renovated theaters when the lights dim, if you have chosen the movie wisely, you can still see star performances.

However, in the eye of my mind, no theater compares to that "smallest theater" of my youth where, following the performance, Mother served homemade root beer and date bars in the living room, turned lobby, for the evening.

FROM SUNRISE TO SUNSET

Utopia is a life of sunrise and sunset with none of the in-between hours.

Sunrise, when the promise and mystery of each day is yet to unfold.

Sunrise, after sleep has refreshed the weariness of the previous day.

Sunrise, when energy is high and the day but a challenge.

Sunrise, when the sun streaked with shades of violet and yellow appears in the east.

Sunset is an even more glorious event. A long Midwestern sunset when the sun slowly goes down on the prairie, when shades of purple and red streak the sky.

Sunset in the Southwest, cut short by mountains, is a riot of red orange framed by cacti.

Sunrise . . . sunset, everyday events which transform each day into a sublime event.

AUTOMATIC WRITING

My pencil writes
of its own direction.
I follow with my thoughts.

SNORING

Most of us don't admit we snore. It's uncouth. Revolting. My husband doesn't snore. I don't. My children don't.

But in the middle of the night or just before dawn, I hear strange noises reverberating throughout our house. I think it is a cat purring louder than usual—until I remember we have no cat. I think it is the television forgotten on after the late night movie. It's not the television. It is my husband snoring.

Recently I purchased earplugs. Fantastic relief except for the fear I won't hear the smoke alarm or, heaven forbid, the alarm clock.

My husband bought earplugs, too.

"Why," I asked, "do you need earplugs?"

His answer astonished me. Angered me.

"Of course, I don't snore."

He convinced me after he recorded strange sounds. I worry I may catch up with my grandma who woke me up in my second floor bedroom (she slept on first floor) with her snoring. In truth, my snoring has begun to wake me up. Even with my earplugs.

A friend and I took a trip and she awakened me every half hour because my snoring kept her awake. Things came full circle because shortly after our trip she married and her snoring was so loud, her husband complained.

Help is on the way. Research on sleep disorder is popular and surgery, hitherto unheard of, is commonplace.

At least the legion of snorers are acquiring celebrity status. One day, I may even toss my earplugs.

YOU'RE STINGY IF YOU . . .

Warm Tuesday's leftover oatmeal
    for Thursday's breakfast.
Dilute the orange juice
    with twice the water.
Encourage your dog to forage
    food from your neighbor's garbage.
Read a magazine when
    checking out groceries.
Wave others ahead of you
    so you can finish the article.
Complain about a 75 percent discount.
Forget to tip the waitress.
Consistently forget to tip the waitress.
Melt soap scraps for liquid soap.
Resole your shoes until the upper cracks
Or your toe peeks through the crack.
Give the same birthday card
    to your husband every year
And the same anniversary card.
After five years, you forget
    what card to use.
And so on—

WAITING

We sit, multi-dimensional,
multi-colored,
multi-troubled,
in the mauve hospital lounge.
Minutes tick to hours,
faces
wear a strained look
expectant of news
about one they love.
My wait is over.
"Everything went well."
The others
still sit with expectant faces,
waiting.

JUST DUMP IT

A dump is preordained to be racing with rats and uninhabitable by humans.

But not always. A dump may be a source of greatest pleasure, as enchanting to a child as a prehistoric dig to an archeologist.

A half mile between my childhood home and our neighbor's was located just such a treasure.

This neighbor had four daughters. The dump provided a depository for broken strings of beads of all colors and shapes, waiting for me to restring. Compacts with mirrors in their lids, empty of powder, and secured with a tiny clasp, held a nickel, a penny and a dime in my pocket.

Cracked plates and cups with intricate designs made great respositories for mud pies and cakes. Buttons abounded.

My four sons clamored to ride to the city dump with their father. They returned with treasures as diverse as a bike with one wheel or an old red wagon. Balls of every shape and size filled the trunk.

A friend frequents the city dump. He drops off something totally useless and returns with furniture to repair or recover. Chairs, needing a new leg or caning, are a challenge. The saw in his shop hums following his frequent trips to the dump.

Spoiling garbage? Rats? No, dumps aren't dismal places. They are a wondrous place for enterprising hunters of artifacts.

THE PAINTING

It is a grim day. My husband's cancer rages as a prairie fire. Everything perishes in its wake.

I dip my brush into the vivid colors of red and purple, making concentric circles with my heart-directed hand.

The painting assumes a life of its own.
I display it, alone, on a white wall.
Most are startled.
"What is this?"
"It's so different from the rest of your pictures."
"I never understand modern art."
"On the weird side, isn't it?"
"Explain it to me."
How do you explain a soul?

ANOTHER MOVING DAY

I belong to a legion of women who arrange and rearrange furniture. Some call it restlessness or an obsessive compulsive act. But, at times, moving the sofa an inch makes all the difference how the room looks in my eyes.

My artist's eye? Or is it an optical illusion?

My husband doesn't notice the difference. Unless his favorite chair is on the opposite side of the room, away from the television. He notices that. Fast. Especially as he sits in mid-air.

"Oops, where did you put my chair?"

Rearranging the furniture is a microcosm of life. Looking for new avenues of change— or escape from the humdrum of everyday life.

Each time I move the furniture, I look at life from a new angle.

GENETIC PHOTOGRAPHY

My father owned one of the few cameras in the area. He took pictures at weddings, funerals and family reunions. He built a darkroom addition to his parents' home where he spent hours immersing film in mysterious solutions.

This interest in photography continued unabated all his life so it was no wonder that I received a Baby Brownie camera in fourth grade. A black and shiny square box, it took tiny pictures. These black and white pictures, most taken in a rural schoolyard, are among my priceless possessions.

A few years later, this first camera was replaced by an Instamatic, a small rectangular camera which recorded pictures from my children's childhood, even more priceless possessions.

Finally, I graduated to a wonderfully complex camera. I learned about zoom and wide angle lenses.

A camera is standard equipment on even weekend vacations. If I pack my lenses in my suitcase, I don't need them. If I leave them at home, they are indispensable.

If I forget my camera at home, I buy a disposable camera at a local drugstore because I see scenery most clearly through the eye of my camera. I don't enjoy the view unless I am composing a picture.

When my grandchildren entered fourth grade, I gifted them a camera with a roll of film, trusting that in time these pictures will become their treasured possessions.

My eldest grandson's maternal grandfather is a professional photographer. His pictures hang at Epcot Center in Florida.

Therefore, with a great-grandfather and grandfather with an enduring love of photography, my grandson's interest in photography as an art form is no surprise. Photography is in his genes.

TREATISE ON T-SHIRTS

T-shirts are the clothing of the 1990s. Big business. Every conceivable (or inconceivable) picture or logo dominates the front and sometimes the back of a shirt.

Grandchildren's faces beam off grandmother's ample chests. Family pictures are printed for a one-time photo look-alike session. Marriages are announced and divorces celebrated on a T-shirt for all to read.

T-shirts come in every size from extra small to extra extra large. Some wear them large as a voluminous tent, whereas others wear them form fitting. They come in average to long and longest lengths—some cover the knees and a few graze the ankles.

T-shirt vendors abound, from parks to football stadiums, from natural disasters such as floods or hurricanes to an unnatural disaster such as a celebrity murder; commemorative shirts sway in the breeze.

Yes, T-shirts are here to stay well into the next millennium, long enough to sport a 2000 logo in bold print.

IN RETROSPECT

Some folks are fast on the trigger with snappy answers, a perfect compliment or a perfect squelch.

Whereas, I think about what I should have said or done—days, even weeks later.

I'd remember to tell my husband, Bill, thanks for making his breakfast every morning and polishing the kitchen after every meal.

I'd thank the paper carrier for placing the paper carefully under the eaves, safe from rain.

I'd double the tip for the waitress the day she ran out the door waving the glasses I had left on the table.

I'd remember to stay calm and reasonable when one of my favorite beliefs comes under verbal attack.

When visiting with a friend, unless asked, I wouldn't offer a solution to her problem. I'd simply listen.

If I received a compliment, I'd smile and say, "Thank you," even if I knew I didn't deserve it.

Most important, I'd tell each of my three sons he is my favorite son.

I'd live with more ease and fewer regrets.

'Tis true.

THROUGH MY WINDOW

Through my window, I see—

    A hummingbird floating on air gathering nectar
    from my red petunias in a millisecond.

    The white sails of the boat skimming
    the waters fifty feet from our dock.

    Colby, the dog next door, the color
    of Colby cheese, ready to play with me.

    Two squirrels racing up the
    oak tree for the sheer fun of it.

    A bluebird sitting on the branch of
    an elm, its feathers shining in the sun.

    The chipmunk scurrying into
    the crack beneath the steps.

    The branches of the maple
    tree swaying in the breeze.

    Grandchildren's footprints on the beach.

JUST ANOTHER DAY

The telephone rang with an urgency that Thelma could not ignore. It was eleven o'clock in the evening and Alfred still wasn't home. She answered the phone with foreboding and heard a well-remembered guttural voice.

"Lady, tell your husband, the cop, to leave us alone or soon his curly black hair will be nailed to the nearest telephone pole."

The line went dead. Thelma's fingers shook as she hung the receiver on its hook.

This Prohibition law isn't working, she thought, as she opened the door to Ilene's bedroom to check if the little two-year-old was covered.

"God, watch over Alfred," she prayed.

God heard and acted. Fast. In ten minutes she heard her husband's key in the front door.

Soon his arms were around her and she told him of the frightening phone threat. He wiped her eyes with his handkerchief.

"Honey, don't worry. I'm careful, you know that. Besides, the rascal who keeps threatening us just wanted to scare you. His bark is worse than his bite."

Thelma smiled. Her husband always used that tired old cliché. She supposed it reassured him. A former schoolteacher, it was comic relief for her to hear it again that night.

Most of Alfred's work as Maryville's only police officer was enforcing an unpopular, unwieldy law. For Maryville was less than two hundred miles from the Canadian border and had become a distribution point for illegal whiskey.

A creek snaked around and through the town. Bottles of booze smuggled from Canada were hidden in its murky waters. Bootleggers had to be well booted to retrieve them.

Alfred took his responsibilities seriously and worked closely with the sheriff and his deputies to catch the rum runners.

Diligent police work had enabled Alfred to discover a cache of whiskey lying half-covered by sand in the creek bed. He turned this evidence over to the sheriff with a description of how and where he found it.

Reassured now that her husband had returned, Thelma changed to her ankle-length white cotton nightgown. Thoughtfully, she slowly fastened the small pearl buttons from the neckline to the hem.

She looked at herself in the mirror on the bedroom wall and was shocked to see the dark circles under her blue eyes.

Too much worry about Alfred and Ilene she thought. She had read about the rash of kidnappings and knew police officers' children were often targeted.

"Alfred, do you think Ilene is safe?" That man sounds like he would do anything . . ." Her voice trailed to a sob.

He put his arms gently around her waist as he led her to their bed and slowly undid the pearl buttons on her gown.

Later, awake, she lay listening to her husband's steady breathing. His revolver and gun belt lay, as usual, on the high dresser by their bed. She hated guns. Always had.

It was, she thought, *a third persona in their bedroom.*

She heard noises outside their window. The usual

night noises were amplified by her fear that the small town of Maryville was turning into a community of random crime.

Thelma felt tired in the morning but busied herself in the kitchen preparing breakfast.

"More bacon, Al?"

"No, thanks."

"Another egg?"

"Too busy to eat more."

"You seem in a hurry."

"Yes, I have two prisoners to transfer to the county jail this morning."

After his second cup of coffee, he strapped on the gun belt, planted a kiss on Thelma's forehead and was out the door.

Thelma washed the breakfast dishes while waiting for Ilene to wake up.

Another phone call. She tensed.

That man again, she thought, drying her hands hastily on the dishtowel.

"Alfred there?"

"No."

"This is Sheriff Peterson. Have him phone me when he returns. Thanks to his lead last week, we caught the ringleaders in the rum runners' ring. In fact, we caught them red-handed."

"Really? That's great."

"Don't tell your husband but we plan to give him the Meritorious Policeman's Award."

"Oh, my, how wonderful, Sheriff."

"By the way, that nut who has been threatening you landed in jail last night so no need to worry about him."

"What a relief. Thanks, Sheriff."

Ilene bounced into the kitchen. She hugged her mother.

"Where's Daddy?"

"He'll be home after awhile, honey. How about some applesauce and toast?"

Thelma thought as she dished the applesauce. *This is just another day in the life of one police officer's family.*

A NEW LIFE UNFOLDING

There is life after retirement. What will you do with it? Amy paged through the *Bridgewater Herald* until the headline in the Life section caught her eye.

About to retire in two months from her position of head nurse on the surgical floor of Mercy Hospital, she started panicking about the future.

Amy Peterson ran a tight floor, respected by medical personnel. True, she had had a few run ins with surgeons on occasion and had fired a few nurses when their asepsis was sloppy or when patients had consistently complained about their nursing care.

Retirement, what next? Working had been an escape for her husband of thirty years had died in a hunting accident. Both her daughters lived in far away places. One a dentist in Chicago and the other a struggling actress in New York City.

She thought, *I have no desire to live in either place. I get lost in Bridgewater, let alone those big cities.*

Amy, who had planned each day so carefully, had neglected to plan for her own future. She had enough money in investments and annuities; therefore, she didn't need to worry about money if she were reasonably frugal. But how to keep busy?

The *Herald's* article suggested a hobby — something you enjoyed doing when you were young. It also suggested exploring new ideas and volunteering. It cautioned if you are thinking of moving to a warmer climate, go visit these places first. Find out which location suits you best.

The article was trite, she thought, as she cut it out and put it into her clipping drawer (the only messy drawer in her house).

Amy sat in her recliner, thinking. She imagined herself in Rome, London, Paris and finally home. She thought of Florida and its ocean breezes and beaches. She thought of the Southwest, Phoenix, Arizona.

That's it! I'll phone Betty, who lives in Mesa and find out more about it.

She dialed information for Betty Loomis's phone number.

"Betty—Amy Peterson."

"Amy—I haven't seen you in over six years. I'm so happy you phoned."

"I'm retiring in two months, and I need direction."

"Are you coming to Arizona? It's a wonderful place to live. No mosquitoes," Betty laughed.

Hearing her friend's joyous laugh reminded Amy of the fun they had always had.

"This is a retirement mecca. Thousands retire here, some come for the winter season, others are year around residents."

"It's a thought."

"Come spend a month, then you can get the feel of the place. I'd love your company."

"Thanks, Betty, I will."

"When?"

"I retire the first of September and I should be able to visit by September 15."

"Let me know and I'll make plans."

"Great. Thanks, Betty, see you soon."

"Bye for now."

Amy felt like a schoolgirl as she hung up the receiver. The two months passed quickly with rounds of retirement parties.

At the last party, a plaque engraved with her name and years of service was presented to Amy. It was to hang in the nurses' station of 3rd floor East. She accepted it with tears of pride and thankfulness for her nursing career. She had planned to be a nurse ever since she had an appendectomy at eight years of age, hospitalized on the very floor where later she became a head nurse.

Amy found it wasn't as difficult to retire as she had thought. Freedom from work with its responsibilities was great and she indulged herself by sleeping until after seven each morning.

A beautiful September day Amy flew from Bridgewater to Phoenix. *Sky Harbor Airport was impressive,* she thought, as she boarded the escalator down to the baggage department. It was such a busy and bustling airport, Amy was happy her friend came to meet her.

The old friends found much to talk about on the drive to Betty's home. They talked until the early morning hours.

In the morning, Betty told Amy to select a grapefruit for breakfast from the tree in her backyard.

The days passed quickly with trips to the Heard Museum, Tallausen, the Botanical Gardens and drives into the desert and nearby mountains.

Strangely, Amy felt as much at home in Arizona as she had in Maine. She decided to spend five months of each year in the Southwest.

Luckily, a mobile home two blocks from Betty was up for sale. The price right, she bought it. It was comfortably furnished and cozy.

A new life unfolding, she thought, *there is life after retirement.*

MY FIRST PRAYER

Now I lay me down to sleep
    Perched on Mama's lap in the white rocker, I repeat it over and over. The first line of my first prayer.

I pray the Lord my soul to keep
    I'm sleepy and mixed up. When I say it the second time, I ask, "Is it keep or take?"

If I should die before I wake
    This scares me a little and I snuggle closer to my mama. I repeat it again and wonder what "die" means. But I don't ask.

I pray the Lord my soul to take
    Which is it, take or keep? Mama's chest is soft and I repeat the prayer.

Now I lay me down to sleep
I pray the Lord my soul to keep
If I should die before I wake
I pray the Lord my soul to take.

    Mama said, as she tucked me into bed and kissed me goodnight, "Now you have memorized your first prayer."
    "Goodnight, Mama."